THE JEWS OF SPAIN AND PORTUGAL
AND THE INQUISITION

GRANT BY FERDINAND AND ISABELLA (AUTOGRAPH), TO A CORDOVA MONASTERY, OF PROPERTY CON-
FISCATED BY THE INQUISITION (VERSO).

THE JEWS OF
SPAIN AND PORTUGAL

AND THE

INQUISITION

BY

FREDERIC DAVID MOCATTA
Late President of The Jewish Historical Society of England

WITH AN INTRODUCTION AND
SUPPLEMENTARY CHRONOLOGICAL TABLES

BY

DAVID BORTIN
of the Philadelphia Bar

ILLUSTRATED JEWISH HISTORICAL SERIES

Edited by I. GEORGE DOBSEVAGE
Formerly Secretary of the Jewish Publication Society of America

A MARANDELL BOOK

COOPER SQUARE PUBLISHERS, INC.
NEW YORK—1973

Originally Published, 1933
Reprinted 1973 by Cooper Square Publishers, Inc.
59 Fourth Avenue, New York, N. Y. 10003
International Standard Book No. 0-8154-0440-9
Library of Congress Catalog Card No. 72-88016

Printed in the United States of America

PREFACE TO FIRST EDITION

The following little sketch was originally composed
as a lecture to some Jewish working-men at the East
end of London. The subject is, to me, naturally an
interesting one no less from a national than from a
family point of view; I hope the Essay may also
prove of some general interest. The position of the
Jews in Spain and Portugal during a greater part
of the middle ages forms an exceptionally bright spot
in their dark and chequered history, and developed
some striking intellectual and moral features in an
age when a great part of what now constitutes Civilisation was wrapped in mental darkness. The
favoured position of the Jews in the Peninsula induced a vast Hebrew population to settle there; and
although it became evident, after a time, that their
prosperity, attracting, as it did, the jealousy of the
bulk of people, would lead to their ultimate ruin,
this could only be effected in a long and gradual
manner, and could only be consummated by a cruel
and violent measure—their forced expulsion.

The struggles of the Mohammedans and the
Christians for supremacy had for centuries excited
the minds of the Spaniards, and imbued them with
a crusading spirit which would tolerate no dissidence
in matters of religion; and this feeling was easily

worked upon by the clergy, in regard to a numerous and thriving community, which remained utterly without the pale of the Christian Church.

Measures of restriction were followed by efforts at conversion on a scale of unprecedented magnitude, till such efforts grew into a persecution, and, still failing to attain the desired end, culminated in the edict of banishment.

Had the Jews possessed more tact during the earlier stages of their troubles, and adhered more closely to their scientific and literary pursuits than to the acquisition of wealth, they might probably have retarded, and possibly have averted, the final doom. It is, however, hardly likely that a population of little less than a million Jews would ever have been allowed to dwell in peace in a land ruled by monarchs as bigoted as Philip II. and his successors, and which almost till our own times permitted a court as arbitrary and as cruel as the Inquisition to hold an undisputed sway. The installation of this Tribunal under Ferdinand and Isabella forms an epoch in the history of Spain, and weighing as an incubus on all freedom of thought and action, was one of the main causes of the decadence of that great country, the effects of which are now so sadly visible. In expelling the Jews, Spain gave the greatest blow to her commerce, as in driving out the Mohammedans she did to her agriculture. Thus, the effects of bigotry and intolerance have recoiled with more lasting evils on the persecutors than on the persecuted; and Spain and Portugal languish, while more tolerant lands have flourished and are continually acquiring strength.

The following are the principal sources from which I have derived my facts:—

GRAETZ. "Geschichte der Juden."

KAYSERLING. "Geschichte der Juden in Portugal."

KAYSERLING. "Ein Feiertag in Madrid."

LINDO. "History of the Jews in Spain and Portugal."

LLORENTE. "Historia de la Inquisicion de España."

HERCOLANO. "Da origem e establecimento da Inquisição em Portugal."

AMADOR DE LOS RIOS. "Estudios sobre los Judios en España."

AMADOR DE LOS RIOS. "Historia de los Judios en España," vols. I. and II.

BEDARRIDE. "Les Juifs en France, en Italie, et en Espagne."

ANONYMOUS (NIETO). "Procedimiento de las Inquisiciones en España y Portugal," etc., etc.

The subject is one which is capable of very considerable elaboration, both as concerns the position and history of the Jews in the Peninsula, and the workings of the Inquisition itself; and I feel that I have rendered but very scant and imperfect justice to a theme at once so interesting and so instructive. I must therefore crave the indulgence of the reader for putting before him a sketch so incomplete, my only excuse being the very limited knowledge of the subject which is generally possessed.

F. D. MOCATTA.

LONDON : *March,* 1877.

INTRODUCTION

The admirable essay by Frederick David Mocatta entiled *"The Jews of Spain and Portugal and the Inquisition"*, which was published exactly fifty years ago and never reprinted, is now made available, because it is still the best succinct summary in the English language of this vital period of Jewish history, an epoch which tested the Jewish soul as nothing has ever done so before or since.

Mocatta's study is a classic. Lord Macaulay praised his style as being of a high order. Its internal merits are attested by translations into several languages and by the fact that it is quoted and excerpted with and without quotation marks. For English readers it has been, in the words of the publishing and book-selling fraternity, "out of print and out of stock", all these years.

It is astonishing how little is known on this side, of the life and work of Frederick David Mocatta (1828-1905), who was one of the most cosmopolitan Jews of his day and who unquestionably occupies a position, not far removed from Sir Moses Montefiore, as a worker for the common good. He was a philanthropist with an unusual sense of the modern preventive method. He combined, not only a comprehensive view of the purposes of philanthropy but made its

scope more extensive by tincturing it with justice
and loving kindness, in the manner of the saints of
his people.

At forty-six he retired from business and devoted
himself entirely to works of public and private benev-
olence. Moreover, he was a patron of learning, in the
finest spirit, and was himself an author of historical
works. It was he who made possible the English
translation of the monumental history of the Jews by
Professor Graetz which was very gratefully acknowledged by the distinguished historian. His popularity
may be judged by the fact that when he reached his
seventieth year he was presented with a testimonial
from more than two hundred national and foreign
philanthropic and literary institutions. That famous
exhibition of Jewish historical and ceremonial objects
held in London in 1887 owed its inception to him.
He was President of the Jewish Historical Society of
England and presented his fine library of rare works
to that organization. It formed the basis of the
Mocatta Library and Museum located at the University of London. To him might very properly have
been applied what Ibn Gabirol said of Samuel ha-Levi
(993-1056), vizier at Granada, that he had worn four
crowns: "The crown of the Torah, the crown of high
station, the crown of distinguished pedigree, and the
crown of good deeds."

Professor Schechter once remarked that he knew a
Cambridge professor who jestingly said that he was
opposed to education for *its own sake*. Mocatta had
an absorbing passion for education. Moreover, he

labored to place the Jew in his rightful position in the world of thought and character. He worked in the schools, he rendered services to Jewish literature, he was a patron of Jewish litterateurs, a veritable worker in the vineyard of the Lord. He loved peace and sought the unity of the brotherhood of man, and aimed to make stronger the golden link which would tie Jew and Christian. It is, therefore, quite fitting that this writing of Mocatta should be brought out again.

History is not only in the habit of repeating itself but often, it contradicts itself. Thus Spain which in 1492 ruthlessly drove the Jews from her dominions became during the World War a land of refuge for many expatriated Jews, among whom was the distinguished Dr. Max Nordau. It was in 1883 that persecuted Jews, driven from Russia, were welcomed enthusiastically in the streets of Madrid, as countrymen returning from exile. In 1913 Joseph and Mary Fels were warmly received by the officials and the citizens of Ronda at the Spanish Land Values Conference held there.

Aside from the historical interest which such a theme holds for the reader (and in the case of the present writer a delightful visit to Spain during 1926, afforded him an opportunity, on the site of the ancient glories, to contemplate the romantic period of our presence on the Iberian Peninsula), there are comparative values to be deduced from a study of the history of a country ''where, ere we were plucked out in anger and in wrath, thrones were set for the Jews, where they rose to be princes and counselors of the land.''

It is the conviction of many philosophic minds that a divine purpose runs through the long trials and sufferings of Israel, and if its tragic history does not contain any inner significance, then the life of man upon this earth has no meaning. For the Jew the rise and fall of Jewish civilization in Spain and Portugal carries with it lessons of tremendous import, especially if he looks forward to a Golden Age of Jewish life in America, in Great Britain and in other civilized countries.

With the settlement of Jews in considerable numbers in any country, possessed with a natural tendency of utilizing all its opportunities, there develops slowly but surely among the so-called native populations a jealousy born of numerous complexes, augmented by ignorance and superstition, which manifest themselves differently in various climes and times. Who would think that even in free America the seed of intolerance would take root in a soil tilled with the blood of heroes and martyrs for the principles of political and religious liberty, equality of opportunity, and universal brotherhood? Who could have foreseen that in this blessed land would flourish defamation and anti-defamation leagues? With a Jewish population constituting but three per cent of the American nation, not to include other equally worthy minorities, who could say restrictions limiting immigration, deliberate exclusion of students from colleges, social separatism, at times violence, evils not conducive to healthy national unity, would take place?

Mocatta, evaluating the tendencies in Spain at the period of the Inquisition, is of the opinion that if the Jews had possessed more tact, adhered more closely to study and spiritual pursuits and had not aimed at security by acquiring wealth, that they might have averted their final disaster. Mocatta, with due respect, is engaged in spinning an "if" of history. With Jews it is rather as in that doggerel:

> You can and you can't,
> You will and you won't;
> You'll be damned if you do,
> You'll be damned if you don't.

Thus, as man can only understand the present by the past and judge the future by correlating it with the present, this little volume may render the double purpose of being not only an historical sketch of a thousand years of Spanish-Jewish history, but serve as a "guide to the perplexed", and be as a column of light for present-day Jewish progress in the lands of so-called opportunity. For it must be remembered that like the Jews of America and the Jews of England who are Americans first, and Englishmen first, Spanish Jews were Spaniards first, who differed only with their neighbors in their creed. Yet the "one hundred per centers" of Spain, the "black hundreds" of those dark centuries, in a most brutal manner made it quite clear to the Jew that he was but an unwelcome sojourner in the "land where his fathers died."

The history of Spain is marked by upheavals as a result of repeated conquests. The first was that made by the Romans after defeating the Carthagenians in the Second Punic War. Spain became a center of Roman culture, producing Seneca, Martial and Quintilian. During the reign of Constantine the Great, Christianity became the ruling religion.

The second important period in Spanish history came with the fall of the Roman Empire, when the Goths assumed supremacy. The Vandals conquered the southern part of Spain naming it Vandalusia (now Andalusia), while other Gothic tribes settled in Galicia and Portugal. These invaders were conquered in 585 by the Visigoths, who in turn were subjugated in 711 by the Moors. The Moorish conquest constituted a complete social revolution in the life of the Iberian Peninsula, for the language and the customs of the Arabs were introduced and superseded all others. Meanwhile, Charlemagne, in the 9th century, conquered Navarre and extended his Empire to the Ebro. In the course of time other Kingdoms, that of Galicia, Aragon, Muncia and Portugal were established. In the thirteenth century greater unity of action among the Christian Kingdoms, and feuds between the Moorish princes led to the latter's disintegration and the loss of power. The Moors were subjugated by Castile and when later in 1469 the Kingdoms of Aragon and Castile were united through the marriage of Ferdinand V and Isabella, the Moors were gradually driven from the field, and soon after abandoned their last stronghold, Granada.

The discovery of America in 1492 extended the Spanish Dominions to Mexico, Central America, South America, while expeditions led to conquest of the coasts of Africa. Asia afforded bases in the Spice Islands and the Philippines, while nearer home its dominion reached out to Navarre, Portugal, Netherland, Naples, Sicily, Sardinia and the Canary Islands. The Spanish Empire girdled the globe and she became the mistress of the world and queen of the ocean.

In 1588 the Spanish Armada was destroyed and with it began the disintegration of the Spanish Empire. This historical résumé is given because as Jews formed a consequential part of the life of the Iberian Peninsula it affected them vitally tossing their destinies with each sweeping tide of fortune.

Mocatta very truly says that there is no reliable historical data to which credence may be given to justify the legends involving Jewish contacts with the Iberian Peninsula, in the time of King Solomon and Nebuchadnezzar. Legend is irresponsible history, yet every folklorist is convinced that back of every tradition there must be at least some foundation of fact. It is known, of course, that the Phœnicians colonized Spain twelve centuries before the Common Era and that they and other Semitic peoples plied their trade to the farthest limits of the Mediterranean and even reached out to the coast of England. It may therefore seem likely that the legends of early visits or even settlements by Jews in Spain are historical events. It is quite certain that the Apostle Paul intended to visit Spain to proclaim Christianity and the

Emperors Vespasian and Hadrian transported Jewish prisoners there. There are references in Rabbinic literature to Spain, while coins unearthed in ancient Sarragosa would indicate the early presence of Jews there. Tombstones, bearing inscriptions of departed Jews antedating 300 C.E., are, of course, further evidence of Jewish life in Spain in the early Christian centuries.

Mocatta, with a true historical sense realizes the importance of the connection between current events and those of the past. He knows that the present is rooted in the past, but he had a definite, limited thesis, and it is left for the historian to cover the field with greater detail. The "Jewish Encyclopedia" under leading articles like, "Spain," "Portugal," "Inquisition," "Moranos," "Auto-da-Fé," "Columbus," and under the various biographies of the notables of Spain and Portugal, has given a great deal of information not available to Mocatta when he wrote his essay. In fact, the remarkable characteristic of his essay consists in its amplitude, for it must be remembered that the researches of Spanish and Jewish scholars, and notably the epoch making works of the great American, Henry Charles Lea, were not accessible to our author.

Neubauer, Jacobs, Kayserling, Kohut, Lea, Medina, Remedios, Marx, Elkan Adler, had not made their researches into Spanish Jewish sources, yet Mocatta's story of the Inquisition, without their contributions, is masterly. Even so distinguished an author as Lea says that there can be no finality in a history resting on so vast a mass of unedited documents. Even he does not flatter himself that he has accomplished such a result though he hopes that he has given a correct survey of one of the most remarkable organizations recorded in human annals. It might be worth while in passing to excerpt from Lea's "Inquisition", volume I, the following paragraph that speaks for itself:

"The annals of mankind afford no more brilliant instance of steadfastness under adversity of unconquerable strength through centuries of hopeless oppression, of inexhaustible elasticity in recuperating from apparent destruction and of conscientious adherence to a faith whose only portion in this life was contempt and suffering. Nor does the long record of human perversity present a more damning illustration of the facility with which the evil passions of man can justify themselves with the pretext of duty, than the manner in which the Church, assuming to represent Him who died to redeem mankind, deliberately planted the seeds of intolerance and persecution and assiduously cultivated the harvest of nearly fifteen hundred years."

And it is no wonder that he holds this view when one finds Nicholas Eymerie ("Manuel des Inquisiteurs," page 142), saying of an Auto-da-Fé that "it is a sight which fills the spectator with terror and is an awful picture of the last judgment. Such fear and such sentiments ought to be inspired and are fraught with the greatest advantages."

It must be remembered that the Doctors of the Church may have been opposed to the Inquisition in varying degrees but primarily they were divided upon the question whether this "heretic" should be put to death by the sword or by fire, or as one authority suggestes, that it does not matter which form of execution is adopted so long as the victim's mouth is stuffed and his tongue tied so that he cannot scandalize the sensibilities of the religious audiences that watch these spectacles. Another church authority, Olonso de Espina ("Fortalicium Fedei," 147 b, printed in 1494) says "that to oppress the Jew is true kindness and real piety, for when the Jew finds that his impiety brings suffering, he will be led to the fear of God and as he who makes another do right is greater in the sight of God than he who does right himself," it is clear why such outrages in the name of God, were glossed over by less learned beings. As Lea further observes, the real importance of the work of the Holy Office is not to be found in the tragedies of the Auto-da-Fé or in the persecutions and its victims, for no matter how numerous these were they were scant compared to the silent influence which the continued and secret labors affected the great masses of the people and the limitations which it placed on the Spanish mind and prevented it later from becoming a part of the progressive world movement which the great revolutions of the last century ushered in. Thus it is not what an individual or a nation does to others that constitutes the greatest tragedy but what it does to its own soul that is the real measure of the disaster.

Because of the limitations of space and also because he is not concerned with the details of the history of the Jews of Spain before the Inquisition, Mocatta finds no need to discuss, or even mention some outstanding personalities and romantic figures of the period. For his purposes the score of Jewish notables and several outstanding renegades were sufficient to fill in the canvass of the panorama he presents.

He gives little space to Spanish-Jewish history under Moslem sway, for he is concerned chiefly with the Inquisition which is primarily a Christian institution. The Jews undoubtedly played important rôles in the transition periods of Spanish history, and the knowledge of the extent to which they supported one cause as against another would be of great historical value. They probably helped ''to make and break'' states. For they were the guides, the counselors, the financiers, and even the soldiers in the armies of the Moors and the Christians—40,000 at one time fighting under Alphonso VI, while the battle of Zallaka was delayed until after the Sabbath was over out of regard to their sensibilities.

It has been found advisable to supplement the essay by Mocatta, to make it even more useful and helpful to students and laymen than it is, by giving a fairly exhaustive list of leading events arranged in a chronological table. Advantage has been taken of the compilations of Lea, Elkan N. Adler and others, to publish as complete a list of such Autos-da-Fé held in Spain where it could be ascertained that one or more Jews were the unhappy victims. The Autos-da-Fé in Portugal were many and even more sombre than those of their Spanish prototype. Lists of these are available but they do not state whether Jews were victimized in them. Therefore only those in which it is definitely known that Jews were participants are given in the list printed in the present volume.

The reader is referred to Lea and Adler for a list of all Autos-da-Fé. To round out the full measure of iniquity, the Autos-da-Fé held in Mexico, in South America, and in some Portuguese provinces have also been appended. One is tempted to suggest that it may with a considerable degree of safety be stated that Jews, in one way or another, did not escape from many of these ordeals.

It is the hope of the writer and all those interested in the search for truth that the several Jewish historical societies of America and Europe may set themselves the task of doing what Jacobs suggested some years ago:

1. The preparation of a ''Corpus Inscriptionum Judaico-Hispaniarum.''
2. The publication of monographs on the social relation of Jews to Christians and Jews to Moors in Spain.
3. The publication of monographs on the rôles of the Jews in the economic and financial development of Spain.
4. Studies on the marks employed to distinguish Jews in different parts of Spain in different epochs.
5. The search for historical and sociologic data to be found in the Hebrew and Arabic writings of Spanish Jews.

Quite a good deal has been written of an Apocri-

phal nature regarding present-day Maranos, but this
much is certain that in many places like Barcelona,
Sardinia, Madrid, Cordova, Toledo and Burgos there
are persons who being conscious of their Jewish
descent are favorably disposed toward Jews, and
similarly the tradition continues in Mexico.   At
Covilha in Portugal there is even at this day a colony
of Maranos.

In the "Machzor Romi," the medieval Italian Jewish ritual, there appears a prayer for Maranos.   It
asks that "God might lead them from oppression to
liberty, from darkness to the light of religion."   Such
prayers usually answer themselves, and it is well that
this is so, for martyred humanity and for that remnant known in history as Israel.

DAVID BORTIN

The following works in addition to those listed by
Mocatta in his Preface, p. vii, are in English and will
be found valuable.

American Jewish Historical Society Transactions,
viii, and Index Volume.

Jacobs, Joseph, "Sources of Spanish Jewish History," London, 1894.

Kohut, George Alexander, "Jewish Martyrs of the
Inquisition in South America," Baltimore, 1895.

Lea, H. C., "History of the Inquisition in the Middle Ages," 1888.   "A History of the Inquisition of
Spain," 4 vols., New York, 1908.

Adler, Elkan N., "Auto de fé and Jew," London,
1908.

"Jewish Encyclopedia," New York, 1901-1905.

ACKNOWLEDGMENT

The reprinting of this essay by Frederic David Mocatta was first suggested by that versatile scholar and exceptional bibliographer, Mr. S. Chait, of New York. He enjoyed the privilege of Mr. Mocatta's friendship and knew the internal merits of the work.

The attention of Mr. David Bortin, of Philadelphia, having been directed to the need of making the study available, readily offered his coöperation and supplied a very helpful Introduction. He also arranged for the preparation of the appended tables and lists. Mr. Bortin's interest in literature generally and in Jewish culture in particular is known and it was indeed a privilege to have this distinguished and scholarly member of the Philadelphia bar associated with the publication.

The Chronological Tables and the Lists of Autos da-Fé were prepared by Mr. Nathan Rosenberg and Mr. Daniel Tapson, both of New York. They gave considerable time to gathering the data and aided in reading the proof.

To these gentlemen the publisher extends grateful acknowledgment.

THE JEWS OF SPAIN AND PORTUGAL AND THE INQUISITION *

The period when Jewish settlers were first attracted to the Iberian Peninsula, where they afterwards attained so high a position in learning and in wealth, and where for some centuries they so thoroughly acclimatised themselves as almost to forget their captivity and to regard themselves as in a new Judæa, is so remote, that no reliable historical data exist on the subject.

No doubt the Phœnicians, at a very early period, traded with the various ports on the Mediterranean, and, as is well known, the Carthaginians—a people closely allied to them in race, and both to them and to the Hebrews in language—founded several cities, and established colonies on the coast. This may probably have given rise to the tradition that Jews were already settled in the Peninsula in the days of Solomon, and that the Tarshish of the Bible was identical with the Tartessus of the ancients, a district of Southern Spain, the principal city of which was Gades, the modern Cadiz. It was also stated that Nebuchednezzar made conquests in Spain, and

* The essay by Mocatta has not been modified in any way, the long paragraphs were left unchanged, even the orthography of the first edition being retained.

1

sent captives from the vanquished kingdom of
Judah to colonise them. These legends, fanciful as
they are, and entirely unworthy of credence, were
studiously kept alive by the Spanish Jews of later
times. Certain it is, however, that Jews very early
found their way to the Peninsula, and that when, on
the fall of the Roman Empire, the Goths and
Vandals conquered the country, large numbers of
them were already established in various districts
throughout the land.

Even under Roman rule the first restrictions
against the Jews were promulgated at the Council
held at Elvira (Iliberis), near Cordova, soon after the
year 300, but the general confusion which followed
the irruption of the barbarians, and the toleration
of the earlier Gothic kings, who were Arians, afforded
a period of comparative repose for more than two
centuries. When, however, at the end of the sixth
century, the Roman Catholic form of Christianity became the recognised religion of Gothic Spain, fresh
edicts of intolerance followed fast from the various
Councils, held principally in Toledo, and soon after,
we begin to hear of those forced, and consequently
feigned, conversions which in later times led to such
sad and disgraceful results. The persecutions became
so frequent and so violent that large numbers of Jews
from Southern Spain sought refuge on the African
coast, and a good understanding arose between them
and the Moors, which the latter used to their advantage when a little later they crossed the Straits
and invaded the Peninsula. The first successful ir-

ruption of the Moslems took place in 711, and such
was the impetuosity of their onslaught, and the dis-
organisation of the Gothic states, that in less than five
years the whole of Spain and Portugal was subjected
to their rule. No doubt the sympathies of the Jews,
oppressed and hunted down under the Goths, were
strongly in favour of the invaders, to whom they were
moreover allied by a kindred monotheistic principle,
and a common Semitic race. At first but tacit spectators of the struggle, they were soon sufficiently admitted into the confidence of the Moslems to be
entrusted with the garrisoning of Seville, Granada,
and other large towns; they were also allowed a per-
fect toleration in the exercise of their religion. It is
asserted, but without sufficient proof, that the Jews
opened the gates of Toledo to the invaders while its
defenders were occupied in celebrating a procession,
on Palm Sunday, in 712. At any rate, it is certain
that the forced converts to Christianity at once returned to their old faith, and that large numbers of
other Jews followed in the wake of the Moslem hosts,
and vastly swelled the Hebrew population of the
Peninsula. Once established on Spanish soil, they
firmly retained their footing, even when, after the
lapse of a few generations, a considerable territory
had been reconquered from the Mohammedans by
Christian valour. Communities of Jews not only
flourished in all the more important towns of Spain
and Portugal, but also established themselves north of
the Pyrenees throughout the South of France. The
new conquests of the Moslems were at first subjected

to the Arab Caliphs of Damascus, but about the year
750, profiting by a revolution in the eastern capital,
'Abd-er-Raḥman I. succeeded in establishing his independence, and governed the country with great wis-
dom and moderation. This monarch founded the University of Cordova, which in the course of a few
generations became, with the schools of Seville,
Granada and Lucena, established by his successors
'Abd-er-Raḥman II. and III., the great seats of the
learning of the day. In order to shed additional
lustre round his new foundation, 'Abd-er-Raḥman
encouraged and invited the presence of numerous
Jewish scholars, who were not slow to avail themselves of the advantages offered. The Jews, notwithstanding the downfall of their nationality, had
preserved their intellectual vigour through the constant and assiduous study of the law of Moses. In
the course of this, they had elaborated the vast codex
of the Talmud, on which they piled commentary
after commentary, holding philosophical disputations on almost every subject relating to physical
science, civil polity, and social economy. These
studies, which saved the Hebrew people from lapsing
into that state of mental atrophy which characterised
what are usually called ''the dark ages,'' were carried
on in the colleges, which they had, in the first
centuries of the Christian era, founded in Palestine,
Persia, and Egypt. The persecutions which raged
in Alexandria, and the fanatical outbursts which
followed the sudden rise of Islamism, had forced the
Jews to close these cherished abodes of learning, and

they were therefore naturally only too pleased to flock
to the new establishments where they had so valuable
an opportunity both of acquiring and of disseminat-
ing knowledge. The Moorish rulers who succeeded
'Abd-er-Ra*h*man I. were equally favourable to Jewish
scholars, and so much interest was excited by Hebrew
literature, that by command of Caliph Hakim, about
the end of the tenth century, Rabbi Joseph Ibn-Abitur
Santos translated the whole of the Mishnah into
Arabic. It would appear, by the names which are left
on record, that by far the greater number of those who
distinguished themselves in these centres of learning
belonged to the Hebrew race. Numerous Jews attained high honour and lasting fame as poets, philos-
ophers, astronomers, physicians, mathematicians, and
grammarians, and many through their linguistic skill
rendered an invaluable service to science and literature, by translating the classical authors of antiquity
into Arabic, while they handed over to the Western
world the treasures of Eastern lore, thus uniting the
whole into one common heritage of human knowledge.

It is a very remarkable fact that, whatever branch
of science or literature was cultivated by the learned
Jews of these ages, the study of their Scriptures, and
of their ancient traditional writings which explained
and illustrated them, always formed the basis of their
mental operations. Deeply versed in Hebrew, the
Jewish authors and poets of the eleventh, twelfth,
and thirteenth centuries resuscitated the language of
their ancestors, and numerous treatises on religious
subjects, on philosophy, medicine, and general science

were produced in classical prose; whilst touching
and beautiful hymns and odes in verse rivalled, in
loftiness of conception and in elegance of diction,
the best periods of biblical composition. Thus for
fully four centuries flourished in Spain, Portugal,
and Southern France, a long list of distinguished
Jewish authors, writing on a great variety of subjects,
generally in Hebrew, but frequently also in Arabic.
The abstruse philosophy of that age has long since
given place to more practical studies, and the
languages employed are too little known in Europe
for the mass of these works to be in any way familiar
even to scholars of our own days. Moreover, in
after ages of bigotry and persecution, a large number
of the writings of these learned Hebrews were
wantonly given over to destruction, both in the East
and West, as being the productions of a hated and
heretical race, so that many of them have been totally
lost. Several of the poetical compositions, however,
still survive in the Jewish liturgy, and are charming
no less from the soul-stirring depth of feeling which
pervades them, than from the elegance of their versi-
fication and their purity of diction.

It may not be out of place here to name a very
few of the more prominent of those distinguished
men, who illustrated not less the race to which they
belonged, than the age and countries which gave
them birth. Among such may be mentioned the poet
and philosopher Solomon Ibn-Gebirol, in the eleventh
century, the poet Jehudah ha-Levi in the twelfth, at
which period also flourished the distinguished family

of Ibn-'Ezra, many of whom held responsible positions in the State, and whose most remarkable member was the grammarian, commentator, and mathematician, Abraham Ibn-'Ezra, who died in 1194. The same century produced the well-known traveller Benjamin of Tudela, and the great Moses ben Maimon, or Maimonides. This extraordinary man (born at Cordova, 1135; died at Fostat, near Cairo, 1204), remarkable alike as philosopher, physician, astronomer, or commentator, is perhaps the greatest illustration produced throughout the middle ages, in any nation, or of any creed. His writings, which are voluminous, and are some in Arabic, and some in Hebrew, exercised a marked determination in forming the mind of his contemporaries, and established a lasting influence on his co-religionists, who have expressed the estimation in which they hold him, in the proverb, "from Moses till Moses, there never was one like Moses."

In the twelfth and thirteenth centuries flourished in Southern France the illustrious family of grammarians, the Kimchis, of whom the best known is David, who died in 1235. Rabbi Moses ben Nachman, or Nachmanides, also in the thirteenth century, was distinguished as a commentator and physician, and Alfonso X. of Castile, surnamed "the Wise," who laid the basis of a new system of astronomy, chiefly availed himself in his researches of the services of Jewish savants, whom he took pleasure in rallying round him.

In the course of a few centuries the Moors were

gradually forced to give up the greater part of their conquests in the Peninsula, first the Northern portions, then Toledo, the whole of Portugal, Valencia, Majorca, Seville, and Cordova, so that they retained, from the middle of the thirteenth to the close of the fifteenth centuries, nothing more than the Kingdom of Granada. At this period a Hebrew population, probably exceeding a million, and forming nearly an eighth of the whole inhabitants, was scattered over the land. This vast aggregate of the Jewish race not only included men foremost in literature and science, and especially valuable for their skill in medicine, but also all those who were best fitted for trade and commerce, and who understood almost by intuition the then little-known rules of finance, and the practical elements of political economy. The great nobles, who, being given up to plans of ambition and to martial pursuits, disdained the details of business, employed the Jews in the management of their vast estates, and thus frequently the thrifty vassals became the creditors to a large extent of their spendthrift lords. The clergy, too, very generally availed themselves of the services of Jews, as the administrators of the enormous landed endowments of which they were possessed, and the kings frequently conferred on them the office of Treasurer; while almost all fiscal charges were confided to their care, and the collection of the taxes, which they usually farmed, was almost exclusively left in their hands.

It is true that the Jews laboured under certain disadvantages; that they had to pay a capitation-tax of thirty-four maravedis, or about eighteen pence, a year; that they were forbidden the use of arms; that they were compelled by law to inhabit a particular quarter of the town, and to wear a distinctive badge on their garments, provisions which, however, they often contrived to elude; and also that, as time went on, restrictive enactments were multiplied and pressed more heavily upon them; but for all this, the Jews became vastly enriched, and acquired so large an amount of power in the State, that it would have been well-nigh impossible to have dispensed with their services. It may easily be imagined that an alien race, devoted to another creed, and possessing to a certain extent an autonomy of its own, a race to which, by its thrift and intelligence, knew how to attract to itself so large a portion of this world's material gifts, would in course of time become the object no less of the dislike than of the jealousy of the great bulk of the population.

The office of tax-collector, however properly administered, has never rendered those who held it very popular, more especially where it has been the practice to farm the taxes. The functions of the capitalists, too, may be indispensable in enabling various trades and enterprises to be carried out, but in circumstances where the lender had so slight a security that the legal rate of interest varied between 20 and 30 per cent., it is easy to understand how those who loaned out their capital could be stigmatised as usurers, and held up to the opprobrium of the very parties who availed themselves of their resources. Moreover, those who allow the accumulation of wealth to form the chief study of their lives, and who flourish on the needs of their neighbours, are sure to fall into a state of mental and moral degradation; and it is likely that the Jews of the Peninsula afforded much colour of truth to the allegation that they were grasping and avaricious. Their natural love of display also caused them, in defiance of sumptuary laws and popular prejudices, to indulge in splendour of domestic arrangements and costume, which still more excited against them the envy and jealousy of those by whom they were surrounded.

It is easy to imagine that the clergy were not slow to avail themselves of the growing unpopularity of the Hebrew race. The pulpits resounded with denunciations and menaces, laws of repression succeeded each other, and every inducement to conversion was offered. Sons of converted Jews were sure of promotion in the Church, then the great highway to all distinction and honour, and inheritance was by special enactments diverted from those who remained steadfast to their ancestral faith, for the benefit of such relatives as adopted the Christian tenets. Occasional outbursts, resulting in pillage and bloodshed, occurred from time to time, from the beginning of the fourteenth century. These hostile demonstrations, which it required all the force of the law to repress, became more violent in intensity, and of more constant recurrence, until they terminated in the final catastrophe of the expulsion.

In 1321 was organised a savage persecution in

the South of France, under the name of the War of
the Shepherds, which, spreading into Northern
Spain, was only put down after much bloodshed by
James II., of Aragon, chiefly by the arms of the
Jews themselves. Soon after this that fearful pesti-
lence called the Black Death, spreading from Asia,
desolated every country throughout Europe, and the
origin of the plague, being inscrutable, was assigned
to the Jews, who, although as great sufferers as
the rest of the community, were accused of having
poisoned the wells. Nevertheless, the wealth and
intelligence of the Hebrews in the Peninsula were
so indispensable that they continued to enjoy the
highest places in the State, which still protected
their worship and legalised the profession of their
faith.

Under Alphonso XI. (1312-1350) and his son
Pedro, surnamed the Cruel (1350-1369), the Jews
enjoyed great favour, and by the latter, Don Samuel
Levi Abulafia was placed at the head of the finances
and, surrounded by a number of subordinates of his
own religion, faithfully performed the duties of his
trust. This officer was permitted to build, at his
own expense, the sumptuous synagogue at Toledo,
now the church of Nuestra Señora del Transito,
which still gives evidence no less of his munificence
than of his consummate taste. After having lived
in a state of unexampled magnificence, he at length
fell a victim to the envy which his ostentation and
pride had excited, and died in prison and under
torture in 1360.

Even Don Henry of Trastamare, who violently wrested the sceptre from his half-brother Don Pedro, found himself obliged to confide many of the highest places of the crown to Jewish hands, and in the neighbouring country, Portugal, the Jews were at the very zenith of their power.

The greater, however, were the worldly fortunes of the Hebrews, the more determined were the clergy upon their fall, and finding that they could make but little impression on the governing classes, they allied themselves with the populace, on whose prejudices and superstitions it was by no means a difficult task to work. The denunciations from the pulpit grew more frequent and more heated, the populace became inflamed, and the Jewish quarters forthwith presented scenes of havoc and bloodshed. No accusation could be too absurd or too improbable to obtain credence: at one time it was that the Jews had blasphemed by cutting in pieces the Host, or consecrated Wafer, when the blood was seen to issue from it, and pour down the streets; at another, it was asserted that they had betrayed mocking gestures while a religious procession was passing; whilst the most frequent and horrible accusation was, that they had stolen and murdered a Christian child for the purpose of celebrating their paschal rites. In consequence of all these allegations the sumptuary laws were again insisted on, obsolete edicts of restriction, dating from the period of the Gothic kings, were brought to light, and the Jews were kept in a constant state of terror, which made their lives a burden

SPAIN IN TH

(Reproduced by permission from

and a continual dread. It must be owned that
among the Jews themselves a state of demoralisation
had set in, and though the tales invented against
them were no less improbable than impossible, it
has been shown that their intense devotion to the
pursuit of worldly gain had induced habits of ostentation, and much lowered their moral and intellectual
status since the days of Maimonides, and of the
scholars of Cordova and Seville. With the exception
of medicine, of which the Jews held almost a mo-
nopoly for many centuries, and in which they were
so distinguished that, amid the most violent persecutions, there was hardly a great personage of Church
or State who did not employ the services of a Jewish
physician, pure science was no longer cultivated.
Philosophy and legitimate Hebrew literature had
given place to the abstruse and often absurd mysti-
cism of the Cabbala, and to the mazy subtleties of
the Sohar; and poetry, no longer aspiring to the
loftiest conceptions, and the greatest elegance, aimed
chiefly at clever conceits, in which alliterations and
acrostics seemed the highest end. Moreover, numerous men of worldly mind, seeing the horizon of their
ambition limited by their religious profession, passed
over to the dominant creed, generally entering the
clerical career as the readiest road to preferment,
and frequently becoming among the most hostile
adversaries of their brethren in race. These men,
armed with their previous knowledge of Judaism
and of Hebrew lore, were employed to refute their
former associates by means of their own weapons,

and wove specious subtleties to prove that the
dogmas of the Catholic Church were established no
less by the Hebrew Scriptures than by the Talmud
itself. Towards the end of the fourteenth century
it became the custom to hold religious disputations
between the clergy (generally converted Jews) and
the Rabbis, and, as is usual in such cases, neither
side being convinced, the doubtful palm was always
accorded to the stronger party, and the Jews were
further stigmatised as obstinate adherents to a proven
fallacy.[1]

The storm which was to culminate in the final
expulsion of the Jews from the Peninsula was silently
but surely gathering. Early in 1391 a fanatical
archdeacon, named Martinez, fulminated a most
tremendous diatribe against the Israelites in the
public square in Seville; the populace, goaded to
phrensy, rushed on the Jews' quarters, destroying,
pillaging, and massacring in every direction, and
when at last by means of the strong arm of the law,
the fury of the marauders was stayed, it was found
that no less than 4,000 Jews had fallen victims in
this barbarous onslaught. Hardly three months
later the same horrid scenes were repeated, and this
time with far more fearful results. The slaughter
was about equally enormous; many succeeded in effect-
ing their escape, whilst numbers were sold into slavery

[1] It is said that these disputations were the cause which led
the Jews to adopt the Christian mode of dividing the text of
the Hebrew Scriptures into chapters and verses, for the purpose
of reference, there being no such division in the original text.

to the Moors, and multitudes sought safety by submitting to be baptised, so that of the 30,000 Jewish inhabitants of Seville hardly any remained.

These terrible atrocities were repeated in numerous other towns throughout Spain—in Cordova, Burgos, Logroño, Barcelona, Gerona, the Island of Majorca, &c. In Gerona the Rabbis assumed a firm attitude, and counselled their brethren rather to abandon life than their ancestral faith; in many places the congregations were fearfully reduced, and in others utterly rooted out. Numbers of Jews migrated into Portugal, where still for two or three generations they enjoyed rest and full toleration, while others sought refuge in the Moorish kingdom of Granada, where liberty of conscience existed to a great degree; but many more ostensibly embraced Christianity, seeking under the shadow of the cross that protection for life, family, and possessions which as Jews could no longer be theirs. The precedent of persons who under violent persecution had outwardly simulated a change of religion, whilst privately following out their own faith, their belief in which remained unchanged, was by no means wanting in the Peninsula. At various periods numbers of Mohammedans had outwardly professed themselves Christians, returning to their own faith when the storm of persecution had passed, and in like manner Christians had often in appearance temporarily embraced Islam to tide over a period of fanaticism, whilst from time to time Jews had been forced on an emergency to put on the garb of either of the dominant creeds, without in any way giving up their inward convictions. Even the great Maimonides himself is said to have been compelled, while wandering in Morocco, to assume, with the rest of his family, the externals of Mohammedanism. His father had removed with his children to Fez, it is thought for the purpose of strengthening his afflicted brethren in their wavering constancy, the Moorish Jews being, at that time, subjected to a most galling persecution. At a later period, when the great philosopher was assailed for his conduct on this occasion, he thought fit to publish a statement, less as a vindication of his own action, than as a guide to other Jews, who might find themselves overwhelmed by a sudden persecution without having the means of escape. The whole story of Maimonides's simulation of Islamism is, however, entirely denied by many eminent Jewish writers, and by such the "Iggereth-ha-Shemad," or Letter on Apostasy, is considered as a spurious document.

Thus at this crisis arose groups of pseudo-converts, whose number, at first limited, became larger by every new outburst of persecution, till, in the early part of the fifteenth century, they were estimated at no less than 200,000. These ostensibly converted Jews were called by their brethren in race "Anusim," or "Forced," and by the Christians "Cristianos Nuevos," or "New Christians," whilst the populace branded them with the name of "Marannos," a word of uncertain derivation, probably a corruption of "Maranatha," and signifying "accursed."

While things were in this state, towards the close

of the fourteenth and rise of the fifteenth century appeared the Dominican monk Vincent Ferrer, afterwards canonised for the result of his missionary labours. This wild fanatic, with a crucifix in one hand, and a scroll of the Law of Moses in the other, thundered out his arguments against the Jewish religion, holding forth sometimes in the open marketplaces, sometimes in the churches, and not unfrequently in the very synagogues themselves. His phrensied ravings terrified the Jews to the verge of madness, and wrought the populace into so excited a state that his discourses were rarely over before the Jews' quarter became a scene of havoc, and multitudes of terror-stricken Hebrews begged for the waters of baptism to save them from imminent destruction. The conversions effected in this manner were really very considerable, but such was the miraculous power with which the Fray Vicente was popularly endowed, that the wildest statements obtained easy credence. He is by some reported to have brought over no less than 35,000 Jews in Salamanca alone, in one year (1411); and it is seriously asserted that he effected 50,000 conversions during the quarter of a century of his preaching.

But St. Vincent Ferrer was not the only adversary to the Jews at this period. Another Dominican monk, Cardinal de Luna, assumed the Papal Tiara, under the name of Benedict XIII., and although he was never recognised as other than antipope by the mass of Christendom, he was supported in his pretensions by the kings of Aragon, and held

his court in grand state at Tortosa in Catalonia from
1412 to 1417. In order to signalise his zeal, and to
insure the support of the clergy, Benedict was violent
in his hostility to the Jews. He and his confidential
physician, a converted Jew, Joshua Lorqui, who had
assumed at the font the name of Geronimo de Santa
Fé, and who was a profound Talmudist, devised a
grand disputation to be held in Tortosa in 1413.
Sixteen learned rabbis were invited to argue on the
tenets of Judaism, especialy as regards the coming of
the Messiah, with Geronimo, and some others, among
whom was Andreas Beltraco, another converted Jew,
and almoner to the Pope, Benedict himself presiding
over the conference. The proceedings were opened in
grand state, with Pope and cardinals, and a vast assemblage of noble and learned auditors, and no less
than sixty-nine sittings were held, extending over a
period of eighteen months, Latin being the language
employed. The first meetings maintained a show of
calmness and dignity, but as time wore on, and it became evident that the arguments on the one side made
no impression on the other, declamation and menace
assumed the place of reasoning, and the conference
broke up in the wildest disorder, it being finally
ruled that the Talmud was a mass of blasphemy and
heresy, which the Jews could no longer be permitted
to use. A string of papal Bulls, offensive and oppressive to the last degree to the Hebrew race, imme-
diately followed, and as a natural consequence a
further large number of pretended conversions took
place. At length in 1417 the great question of the

papacy was set at rest, Benedict XIII. was deposed, deserted, and left to die in obscurity, and Martin V., a pontiff who appears to have been favourably inclined towards the Jews, was universally recognised as the successor of St. Peter. But the harmful influences thus powerfully set in motion could not be lulled to rest; the Church teemed with converts from Judaism, who sought to show their zeal by the oppression of their former brethren. Among these Paul de Sta. Maria, Bishop of Burgos, and his sons, one of whom was Bishop of Cartagena, and Alfonso de Espina, who became Rector of the University of Salamanca, notably distinguished themselves, and fanned the flame of persecution which the populace were only too ready to keep alive.

While matters were in this threatening position in Spain, alarming indications showed themselves in the western kingdom of the Peninsula. In Portugal the position of the Jews had hitherto been highly favoured; as in Spain, they were liable to certain disabilities which were not very rigorously enforced. They dwelt generally in separate quarters, and were nominally subject to sumptuary laws as to apparel, &c., but they were internally governed by their own regulations, their counsels being presided over by their Chief Rabbi, while frequently many of the highest offices in the State were confided to members of their body. The Chief Rabbi (*Arrabi-Mór*) was always appointed directly by the Crown, and so important was deemed the post that the filling-up of a vacancy in the office, which occurred in 1384, gave

rise to a court intrigue, the effects of which exercised
a lasting influence over the destinies of the country,
and became the main cause of placing Don John of
Aviz on the throne of Portugal, and averting the
threatened fusion of that kingdom with Castile.
The wealth and position of the Jews, added to their
inordinate love of display and supercilious manners,
had long rendered them unpopular, and the recent
persecutions in Spain had tended to vastly increase
their number in the sister country, whilst the clergy
studiously favoured the growing aversion, which first
terribly exploded in Lisbon in December, 1449. The
outburst appears to have originated in a street riot,
in which several Jews were insulted and maltreated,
and on their offering resistance the mass of the
populace precipitated itself on the Jews' quarter,
crying out: "Murder them, pillage them!" Acting
in the spirit of their words, the rabble ransacked the
whole district; many Jews were killed, and more
were wounded, and it was only through the efforts
of the military, and by the personal intervention of
the king (Alfonso V.), who hurried to the capital,
that order was at length restored. The condition of
the Jews in Portugal was visibly growing worse, yet
for more than forty years no open outburst of persecution is recorded, and many high offices still continued to be confided to them. The brothers Ibn
Jachia, who belonged to a long line of counsellors
and physicians, still maintained those charges at the
court of Alfonso V. Abraham de Beja and Joseph
Zapateiro were commissioned to accompany the

DETAIL OF DECORATIONS ON THE WALLS OF THE FOURTEENTH
CENTURY SYNAGOGUE AT TOLEDO

voyage of discovery to the East Indies; and the names of other Hebrews are also found in prominent places. Moreover, though the Jews of Portugal hardly attained as high a position in learning as their brethren in Spain, Hebrew literature was largely cultivated, and in the reign of John II., Hebrew printing was introduced into Portugal, and continued up to the year of the expulsion, exhibiting a very great perfection. But the man who shed the greatest lustre over the declining period of the Jews in the Peninsula was Don Isaac Abravanel (b. 1437, d. 1509), of a family which, descended from the royal house of David and lately immigrated from Spain, had already through several generations distinguished itself by its attainments, and was destined to enjoy in other lands an honourable succession for nearly a couple of centuries. This great man was for many years Minister of Finance, and confidential counsellor of the king. Endowed with wonderful mental abilities, and with a determination to achieve greatness, gifted by nature with a remarkable power of acquiring influence over other men, and with a rare desire to benefit others through his own advantages, Abravanel became no less the friend and adviser of his sovereign than of those royal and noble personages who formed the Court, avoiding with the rarest tact those difficulties and jealousies to which his exalted position rendered him eminently liable. Possessed of large wealth, he was munificent in acts of charity, a notable instance of which occurred on the taking of Arzila, a port on the African coast, by the Portuguese, on which occasion 250 Jewish captives were sold into slavery. Abravanel subscribed largely to purchase the freedom of these unfortunate persons, and collected from his wealthier brethren, both in Portugal and in other lands, sufficient funds not only to place them in liberty, but also to provide for their future necessities. Deeply imbued with the love of Hebrew literature, he gave up his hard-earned leisure to serious studies, and commenced amid the cares of business and the toils of State a learned commentary on the law of Moses, and other portions of the Bible, and several philosophical works, tasks which, carried on through all the vicissitudes of his career, were only brought to a close at a later period of his life, when exile gave him comparative repose. At the death of his great friend and protector, Alfonso V., in 1481, and the accession of his son John II., the whole of the courtiers of the late king were disgraced, and Abravanel with difficulty succeeded in eluding the pursuit of the new sovereign, who confiscated the whole of his vast estates. Reduced to poverty he managed to escape into Spain, where he joined Don Abraham Senior, the great farmer of taxes in Toledo, who admitted him into partnership, and thus enabled him to re-construct his ruined fortune. He now pursued his studies with unremitting zeal, terminating some of his earlier works, and publishing some very original and valuable commentaries on the prophetical and historical books of the Bible. We shall presently see how he nobly came forward to endeavour to avert the doom of expulsion from his brethren in Spain, foiled in which he fled to Naples, where he was hospitably received by the King, Ferdinand I. On the death of this sovereign Abravanel accepted office under his son and successor Alfonso II., and when that prince was shortly afterwards forced, through the irruption of the French, to abdicate in favour of his son, and to flee to Sicily, he accompanied him thither. His family, however, were dispersed in flight, and the infant child of his eldest son Judah, himself a very distinguished man, was kidnapped by the King of Portugal, and forcibly brought up in the Christian faith. Alfonso died in 1495, when Isaac Abravanel fled to Corfu, whence he afterwards returned to Monopoli, near Bari, and finally betook himself with the remnant of his family to Venice, where he died in 1509. Meanwhile things were tending to a crisis in Spain, where edict followed edict, to embitter the lot of the Jews, and in 1474 Ferdinand and Isabella succeeded to the united crowns of Aragon and Castile. The creation of so important a monarchy inspired no less ruler than subjects with the dominant desire to bring under the same sceptre those provinces of southern Spain, which, though tributary since 1244, were still governed by the Mohammedan kings of Granada, and thus subjecting the whole country to Christian rule. The King was ambitious, unscrupulous and avaricious to the last degree; the Queen, though possessed of many womanly virtues, was superstitious, and entirely in the hands of the priests, and both entered warmly into the new crusade. At such a juncture, when religious feeling was so excited, it was not likely that the Hebrew race, as much an object of aversion from the obstinacy with which it rejected Christianity as of jealousy on account of the vast wealth which it had accumulated, would meet with much toleration. The sect of New Christians had been rapidly growing, and as it increased, the line of demarcation between them and the ''Old'' Christians had become more marked, so that it was now hard and fixed, and as it became evident that the Christianity of the neophytes was little more than a pretence, their condition was but slightly improved by their apparent conversion. It is true that the converts ostensibly conformed to the tenets of the Catholic faith, assuming fresh names, filling their houses with crucifixes, images of saints, and other symbols of Christianity, and regularly attending the services of the Church; but these new habits sat uneasily on them. It is by no means difficult to imagine that persons, brought up in a faith which they were forced to abandon through fear or worldly interest, would not in their hearts be very zealous in their attachment to the religion which they were constrained to adopt. In secret they observed as many of the practices of Judaism as they were able to do without fear of discovery, studiously inculcating Jewish notions into the minds of their children, and endeavouring by every means in their power to keep alive in their descendants the memory of the old religion. Thus they led, as it were, lives of perpetual deceit, and ill at ease within themselves, were ever silently praying that their conformity to practices, which appeared to their mind but little less than idolatry, might not be accounted to them as mortal sin. It was therefore, in a great number of cases, easy to obtain proofs that the New Christians were by no means purified from their old errors and superstitions, and thus their assumption of the dominant faith did not long shield them from the violence of the populace. Hence we hear of persecutions specially directed against the New Christians, in Valladolid, in 1470, in Cordova, in 1472, and so on, during the next twenty years, in various other towns.

The relations between the converts and their former co-religionists appear to have been of the most intimate nature: ties of blood, and feeling, and a strong bond of commercial interest, created a powerful link between those Hebrews who had placed themselves without the pale of Judaism, and those who still remained within. The latter appeared to recognise in the defection of the former the inevitable force of circumstances, and sought to aid the "Anusim" by all means in their power, to keep up the clandestine exercise of such rites of Judaism as they still contrived to practise. Thus the Jews still more drew upon themselves the animadversion of the clergy, and gave rise to a future source of accusation, that of being guilty of "Judaising," for which they were about to suffer in a terrible manner.

Matters were evidently growing to a climax; and the materials for the great act of state-policy, which was to purge Spain from the stigma of Judaism, were only waiting some bold master-hand to combine them and give them full force. Such soon arose in the person of Fray Tomas de Torquemada, a Dominican monk, who had been confessor to the Queen in her younger days, and who was possessed of an iron will, joined to great mental power, and an unflinching pertinacity of purpose. For the carrying out of his ideas, the creation of a great religious and political engine, which would become their legal embodiment, was absolutely necessary, and accordingly he laboured with all the energy of his nature to procure the establishment in Spain of the Court of the Inquisition. This tribunal had originally been devised to crush the heresy of the Albigenses early in the thirteenth century, by Fray Domingo de Guzman, better known as St. Dominic, who obtained from Pope Innocent III. (in 1212) the title of Inquisitor-General. It first began its career in Sicily, whence it shortly extended to other states of Italy, to Southern France, Catalonia, and afterwards to Aragon, in which kingdom from time to time heretics were given over to the flames. Castile and Portugal were also to some degrees under its influence, but as the heresies which called it forth no longer could be said to exist, and the Church of Rome held undisputed sway over Western Christendom, the Inquisition, by the middle of the fifteenth century, had become generally a languid institution, and in most countries had already ceased to be.

It might easily have been thought that at the

TORRE DEL ORO, SEVILLE

period when the revival of letters, the invention of printing, and the discovery of America gave a new tone to human thought, and opened fresh avenues to public and individual enterprise, this organisation for diving into the minds of men and watching the habits of their privacy, in order to guard against any original speculation on matters of belief, would have died out, scared away by the day-light of advancing civilisation. Unfortunately, the very reverse occurred, and the institution became re-organised and intensified at the precise juncture when it might naturally have been expected to become extinct. It so happened that in 1477 Philip de Berberis, Inquisitor of Sicily, which formed part of the dominions of Ferdinand, came over to seek the confirmation of a privilege accorded by the Emperor Frederic II., in right of which one third of the possessions of condemned heretics became the property of the Inquisition; and this iniquitous system having received the royal sanction, it became evident how magnificent a prey would be ready to fall to a similar institution in Spain, could such but obtain a legal establishment. Fray Alonso de Hojeda, prior of the Dominican convent in Seville, and Nicholas Franco, the papal nuncio, exerted all their energies to this end, and succeeded in obtaining from Sixtus IV., in 1478, a Bull authorising Ferdinand and Isabella to choose sundry archbishops, bishops, and other persons, clerical and lay, for the purpose of conducting investigations in matters of faith, and proceeding against heretics and those who protected them.

Ferdinand entered readily into a scheme which promised such brilliant results to his cupidity; but the Queen hesitated to sanction in Castile the establishment of a tribunal which not only threatened proceedings of a most vexatious and cruel character, but which was odious to the greater part of her subjects, and disliked even by a large portion of the clergy. It was at first sought to temporise; Cardinal Mendoza, Archbishop of Seville, published a special catechism for the use of the New Christians, and various other methods were adopted in order to avert the threatened crisis, but the Dominicans were not to be thwarted. Alonso de Hojeda, Fernando de Talavera, confessor of the Queen, and afterwards Archbishop of Granada, Diego de Merlo, Pedro de Solis, and other priestly personages in favour at Court, headed by Torquemada himself, whose influence was unbounded, never for a moment relaxed their energies. They constantly represented to her the wickedness of the "evil seed of Israel," the blasphemies they were ever uttering, the intrigues they were ever weaving, and the impiety they were ever practising under the veil and cover of their assumed Christianity. Such arguments could not fail to triumph in the end, when addressed to a weak and superstitious woman like Isabella, and in September 1480 she reluctantly and tremblingly affixed her signature to the document which established the Inquisition in her dominions. Soon afterwards Fray Tomas de Torquemada was created Inquisitor-General, the convent of St. Paul, to which was shortly added the castle of Triana, in Seville, was given up as the first seat of the Tribunal, and a field adjoining was appointed as a Quemadero, or burning-place for heretics, a spot marked by a square stone pavement, with a colossal statue of a prophet at each corner, and which retained its name down to the commencement of the present century.

The opening of the year 1481 saw the installation, in its more extended and terrible form, of that horrible court, which stands unequalled for acts of atrocity perpetrated in the name of religion, and which, under the pretext of purging Spain from heresy and Judaism, gradually involved the whole country in ruin, from which it has never been able to recover. Since the Church claimed no jurisdiction over acknowledged Mohammedans or Jews, and since accusations of heresy and witchcraft were at this period by no means frequent, the whole force of this new and tremendous engine was directed against the Marannos or New Christians. Frightened out of their senses by this terrible apparition, vast numbers of these unfortunate people fled from Seville, seeking refuge with the Duke of Medina Sidonia, the Marquis of Cadiz, and other great nobles, whose almost sovereign position in their various domains was thought to be able to afford protection from the impending storm. Hospitably received as they were, their flight proved of no avail, for the first edict of the new court was to summon all nobles, barons, and feudatories to send back all the fugitives to Seville within a fortnight, under pain of deprivation of their titles and honours, and sequestration of their estates. Within four days of the installation of the Inquisition took place the first *auto-da-fé*, or Act of faith, when six persons perished in the flames. In March, April, and November followed fresh human sacrifices, to such an extent that, in the first year, 298 individuals were burned, and in the second, no less than 2,000; besides which 17,000 persons were subjected to do penance, involving either total or partial loss of their property, and the disgrace of themselves and their families.

The large scale of the proceedings of this second year (1482) was no doubt induced by an artful snare, devised by the Inquisitors to entrap the largest possible number of the converts. This was the issuing of an "Act of Grace," by which within thirty days all those New Christians, who had been guilty of practices denoting a relapse into Judaism, were summoned to come forward and declare themselves, and holding out the assurance of full absolution, and the preservation of their lives and property, to all such as were contrite and promised amendment.

Numbers of the unfortunate Marannos were lured by this "Edict of Grace," and consequently the Tribunal became possessed of a register of the suspected, which was indefinitely enlarged, as none who made confession were allowed to depart until they had given a list of all those of their relations or acquaintances who might possibly be guilty of a similar relapse,—a plan which afforded in many instances a fruitful means of gratifying private malice and personal vindictiveness. The individuals thus named were, on the expiration of the term of the "Edict of Grace," ordered to present themselves within six days, and if they refused to comply, they were taken by force from their houses and lodged in the dungeons of the Inquisition.

It is interesting to know what were considered as proofs of a relapse into Judaism. Thirty-seven articles were drawn out, and the mention of a few of them is sufficient to prove how frivolous and absurd were the grounds, which sufficed to deprive multitudes of unfortunate fellow-creatures of happiness, property, and life. It was to be investigated whether an individual had made a difference between Saturday and other days, by laying a white cloth on the table, or putting on a clean shirt, or better clothes than on other days; whether he had cut the throat of a fowl in killing it for food, or had withdrawn the sinew from an animal destroyed for the same purpose; whether he had eaten meat during Lent, or on the Fasts prescribed by the Church, or had abstained from food on the Jewish day of Atonement, or other Hebrew Fasts, or had used baths, cut his hair, or pared his nails on days preceding such Fasts, or had eaten unleavened bread, or used certain herbs in Passover, or procured green branches, or made presents of fruit to friends at the time of the Feast of Tabernacles, or drunk "Casher" wine (that prepared for Jewish ceremonials), or eaten meat killed by Jews, or repeated certain Jewish blessings on particular occasions, or recited the Psalms of

David without concluding with the words "Glory be
to the Father, and to the Son, and to the Holy
Ghost"; whether any parent had given Hebrew names
to his children, or washed or shaved the head of a
child on the part on which the chrism of baptism
had been poured, or invited his friends and relations
to dine before leaving on a long journey, or whether
a dying man had turned his face to the wall, or had
it so turned by others, or a dead body had been
washed in warm water, or the water had been
emptied out from all vessels in the house of a deceased
person, together with a long catalogue of similar
enquiries.

Such were among the proofs of relapse from the
newly adopted faith into the errors of the old superstition. Sad indeed was the fate of those, of whom
it could be pretended that they cooked their stews
in oil instead of lard, and many Old Christians in
after times had to repent that their casual dislike to
pork or shell-fish had brought them under the suspicion of being secret votaries of what it pleased the
Inquisitors to designate as "the impious law of
Moses."

By such means and by the agency of the machinery
which is about to be described, it is certainly not
surprising that the victims of the Inquisition were
no longer counted by hundreds, but by thousands,
and tens of thousands, especially as the tribunal
established in Seville was only the prototype of
numerous other similar courts instituted in all the
large cities of Spain: Toledo, Cordova, Ciudad Real,

Saragossa, Valencia, Barcelona, Madrid, Salamanca, Valladolid, Segovia, and various other places, all could boast of their courts of Inquisition, their dungeons, and the Quemaderos, which, established generally despite the most lively opposition of the inhabitants, grew to be regarded in after times as fixed institutions.

In Aragon the creation of the New Tribunal was so unpopular, that a plot was laid against the first inquisitor in Saragossa, Don Pedro de Arbues, who, though he was made aware of the conspiracy, and consequently wore armour beneath his clerical habit, was smitten down and killed in the cathedral of that city in September, 1485. As is the usual result of crimes of this description, a revulsion of feeling followed, with a persecution of the New Christians, who were accused of having instigated the deed. The Aragonese Inquisition became an accomplished fact, and the slain Inquisitor at a later period received the beatification of the Church.

It may easily be imagined how the new proceedings inspired fear far and wide, when it is considered that not only some hundreds of thousands of the population were known to belong to the New Christians, but also that by intermarriage with the converts vast numbers of the people, largely including the highest nobility and clergy, were the descendants of Jews, and were consequently amenable to the proceedings of the dreaded tribunal. Many of the more sober-minded Spaniards saw with horror the extent to which this abuse of power was carried, and, joining

in a common protest, petitioned the Pope for a cur-
tailment of the functions of the new magistrates; the
New Christians supported the petitioners by the
more forcible arguments of their gold, and vast
were the sums sacrificed to obtain Bulls for the miti-
gation of the severity of the courts. In the first
instance the result was successful, and Sixtus IV. in
1482 issued a Bull blaming the indiscriminate zeal
of the Inquisition; but Ferdinand was inexorable,
and by means of lavish gifts he extorted from this
Pope, and his successors Innocent VIII. and Alexander VI., fresh powers confirming the Tribunal in
the full exercise of its office.

Anxious to give a precise legal embodiment to
the institution, Torquemada and his associates drew
up an elaborate code of twenty-eight articles, or
constitutions, defining the duties and aims of the
Holy Court in the following manner. After announcing the establishment of the Inquisition in
Seville, and decreeing the institution of similar
courts in various towns throughout the country, the
Edict of Grace was set forth, inviting heretics and
Judaisers within thirty days to come to declare
themselves, and to denounce all others whom they
knew to follow similar practices. Those who volun-
tarily came forward and confessed within this term
were subjected to fines in money, and to the ceremony of a public absolution, which involved the
deprivation of titles and honours, and rendered the
absolved ineligible for all offices of public trust; a
"re-habilitation" was, however, in some instances

procurable at the expense of a large portion of their fortunes. No absolution was granted unless the persons who claimed it not only penitently confessed their transgressions, but also furnished a list of all those whom they believed to be guilty of similar relapses. Against all those who did not offer their confession within the thirty days assigned, the entire confiscation of their property was decreed. For this purpose their possessions were assessed, not at the date of their accusation, but at that of their assumed committal of the crime of heresy, so that if they had made them over to other hands, they were to be restored to the Inquisition. Persons under twenty years of age, who pleaded that they had been led into error by their parents or guardians, were to do penance by being condemned to wear during one or two years the disgraceful garb of the Sanbenito, in which they were to appear in all church ceremonials.

The Sanbenito (or saco bendito), which we shall often have occasion to mention, as figuring in acts of penance and in ''acts of faith,'' was a cloak of coarse serge, which varied in form and in design at different periods. The garment covered the whole body, and was yellow in colour, with flames, demons, serpents, and crosses painted on it in red, and arranged according to the delinquency of the wearer. With the Sanbenito was worn the ''coroza,'' or high-pointed cap, made of a like material, and covered with similar devices, and generally bearing on its front a placard, on which were written the name and offences of the wearer.

Those who were committed to the dungeons of the court with a view to their being handed over to the secular arm, for capital punishment, as impenitent, and who afterwards declared their repentance, obtained the commutation of their sentence to imprisonment for life in the cells of the Inquisition. Those who remained impenitent, or who relapsed from their penitence or were supposed to have made a feigned confession, were handed over to the secular arm to be committed to the flames. Such as refused to confess, or were suspected of having made only a partial confession, were to be subjected to torture, which was to be administered under the eyes of two Inquisitors, or, where such could not attend, of their appointed delegates, who were to conduct the interrogations, and to take down the depositions of the accused. In cases where such confessions were afterwards retracted, as naturally often happened, a fresh application of torture might be made, and though this second infliction was at a later period pronounced illegal, the effect was the same, since the procedure was merely declared to be ''suspended,'' and the prisoner was subjected to its continuation at a subsequent period. Those who, being accused, were able to elude the officers of the tribunal, were considered condemned by default, and were deprived of their property, and often burned in effigy. A deceased person, against whom an act of heresy could be proved at any period subsequent to 1479, was condemned to have his body exhumed and burned, and all the property he had left was to be

taken from those who had inherited it, provision
only being made in these, as in other cases of confiscation, that children under age, who were thus
disinherited, should be brought up on some small
provision allowed by the State, and duly educated in
the Catholic faith. All inheritances derived from
persons who had incurred condemnation were declared invalid and forfeited to the Crown. The Inquisition claimed full jurisdiction over all seignorial
domains, as well as over the Crown lands, and was
free to form such establishments as it deemed necessary throughout the whole country. Lastly followed
certain clauses concerning the discipline of the Inquisitors themselves, adjuring them to live in peace with
each other, prohibiting them from receiving presents
or bribes, and enjoining that all disputes which might
occur between them were to be settled in secret
by the Inquisitor-General, without reference to the
bishop of the diocese or to the ecclesiastical courts.

Besides the foregoing, eleven additional acts were
promulgated relating to the internal government of
the tribunal, defining the duties of the Inquisitor-
General, of the various Inquisitors throughout the
provinces, of the registrars, secretaries, legal officers,
alguazils, and of the vast assemblage of subordinate
officers, who were afterwards known as the "familiars
of the Holy Office." Moreover, a resident at the
Court of Rome was appointed to represent the Inquisition at the Papal See.

Such form the bases of the constitution of that
celebrated tribunal which was, for more than three

centuries, to place its iron hoof on the liberties of the nation, crushing out all freedom of human thought, and reducing the minds of men to one dead level of stagnant uniformity. With so terrible an engine invented specially for their destruction, it is not wonderful that the New Christians should become panic-stricken, and, leaving their homes in despair, should seek refuge in other lands. Their former Hebrew brethren in faith, trembling for their own fate, liberally assisted them for this purpose, and tens of thousands poured out of Spain, the greater part flocking into Portugal, many into the still Mohammedan kingdom of Granada, while others sought a refuge in Italy, and even in Rome itself. But since the year 1481, Ferdinand and Isabella had been strenuously prosecuting their campaign against the Moors in the south, and at length, after more than ten years of arduous struggle, the war ended in the triumph of the Christian arms; the Moorish King, Abdallah, or Boabdil, submitted, his capital, Granada, surrendered, and by the opening of 1492 the Moslem rule in the Peninsula had disappeared for ever, and Ferdinand and Isabella became undisputed monarchs of the whole of Spain.

While the sovereigns, elated with their recent success, were still at Granada, surveying from the Alhambra the crests of the snowy Sierra, with the fertile Vega at its base, and the rich and vast territory which they had won, no less for themselves than for Christendom, the Inquisitors brought to bear on them all the sophistry of their arguments to

carry out at this favourable juncture the long con-
ceived and desired project of the expulsion of the
Jews from Spain. The plan was by no means without a precedent; in 1290 Edward I. had, without
consulting parliament, banished the Jews from
England; in 1306 Philippe le Bel pronounced their
first expulsion from France, their final exile, after
having been recalled, being effected by Charles VI.
in 1394; they had been also expelled at various
periods from most of the states of Northern Italy,
and from Sicily, as also from various states of Ger-
many.

The Hebrew race, as has been seen, had very long
been an object of intense jealousy and superstitious
aversion in Spain, and probably the popular antipathy, coupled with the anticipation of the speedy
reversion to themselves of the huge wealth of the
Jews, which it would be quite impossible that they
could carry away with them, acted as powerful in-
centive towards the consummation of the measure.
Torquemada, as may readily be supposed, was an
earnest supporter of the project; his wrath had
always been rabid against the insincerity of the New
Christian, and the secret communications which
they maintained with the Jews had further incensed
him against the hated race. Moreover, he had re-
cently insisted on the deposition of two bishops, sons
of converted Jews, because they had refused to
authorise the bodies of their fathers to be taken
from their graves, upon a demand which had been
made under the pretext that they had died in heresy.

He had also attempted to compel the Rabbis of
Toledo to give up upon oath the names of all those
converts to Christianity who still practised Hebrew
rites, a demand which was bodily refused.

In order to prevent all connivance between the
Jews and the Converts, Torquemada made a firm
resolution never to cease from his efforts till he had
succeeded in the design of driving all the former
from the realm, a project in which he found but
little resistance from Ferdinand.   That prince,
though mainly relying upon Jewish capital for the
prosecution of his wars against the Moors, had never
disguised his antipathy to the Hebrew race.   On the
taking of Malaga in 1487 he had caused twelve New
Christians who had fled thither and resumed their
old faith to be transfixed with lances, and had sold
450 Jewish captives, mostly women, into slavery,
from which they were nobly ransomed by Don
Abraham Senior for the sum of 20,000 doblas of
gold.   The assent of Isabella was less easy to obtain,
for she always evinced an under-current of feeling
which made her at first recoil from sanctioning acts
of cruel and oppressive persecution.

The force of bigotry and fear, and the distorted
reasoning of the Inquisitors, proved however too
strong for any sentiment of compassion, and on
March 31, 1482, went forth the fatal edict enjoining
that all non-baptised Jews must quit the whole of
the Spanish dominions, including the islands of
Sicily and Sardinia, within the space of four months.
The proclamation was based entirely on the grounds

that the Jews were proved guilty by the Inquisitors and others of perverting Christians to their own belief, and spreading among them the knowledge and practice of Jewish rites and ceremonies. It stated that originally it had been contemplated to limit the measure to the expulsion of the Jews from all the cities and places in Andalusia, but that it had been found necessary to extend it to the whole country. Despite the ordinances which had been passed for preventing communication between Jews and Christians throughout the land, the former had continued to use every means in their power to subvert the holy Catholic faith by endeavouring to bring over faithful Christians to the observances of the law of Moses. It was thus deemed absolutely imperative, after mature deliberation, to banish the Jews from the whole kingdom, and accordingly they were all ordered to depart, never to return, before the end of the month of July in the current year, 1492. All such as remained after that date incurred the penalty of death, and of confiscation of their entire property to the royal treasury. All persons, of whatever rank, who harboured any Jew or Jewess after that date, were to forfeit their estates or property. The edict concluded by a promise of royal protection to the Jews during the remaining four months, with permission to travel in safety, and to sell, alienate, or otherwise dispose of all their movable or immovable property. They were also to be allowed to export their wealth and substance either by sea or land,

with the exception of gold, silver, or other articles
prohibited by law.

It may be deemed highly creditable to the Jews
that the accusations brought against them were
strictly limited to their wishing to bring over
Christians to Judaism, a charge which could only
have been meant to apply to the New Christians,
who were in reality Jews themselves. The then
prevalent and favourite accusations that the Hebrews
were given to practices of usury and false dealing,
that they had abducted and crucified Christian
children, had desecrated the Host, or had poisoned
large numbers of the population in the course of
their extensive medical practice, might not unnaturally, have been expected to find a place in the
document; to none of these subjects, however, was
the slightest allusion made, although the Inquisitors
were industrious in circulating all these charges in
justification of the measure.

This remarkable and final edict, although it
might have been seen looming in the distance for
many years, fell like a thunder-bolt on the Jews.
To be forced to quit the soil which their ancestors
had inhabited for so many centuries, which they
loved as no other land had been loved by Israelites
since the destruction of Jerusalem, to abandon those
many relatives, who though they had nominally
quitted their faith, still remained Jews in feeling,
and who were now to be handed over to a ruthless
persecution, to exchange the wealth which they had
so long enjoyed for poverty and exile, was too bitter

GARDEN AND HOUSE OF SAMUEL HA-LEVI, AT TOLEDO,
FOURTEENTH CENTURY.
(From a photograph taken in 1926, by David Bortin, of
Philadelphia)

a thought for endurance. Great was the interest used, and vast were the efforts made to avert the fatal decree. The Jews offered to submit to any terms, and to sacrifice any amount of treasure, merely to be permitted to remain on Spanish soil.

At this crisis that grand and remarkable character, Don Isaac Abravanel, who, as we have seen, had long been established at Toledo, stepped boldly forward, and accompanied by some of the more notable of his co-religionists, threw himself at the feet of the King and Queen, offering to raise 300,000 ducats, provided the decree were revoked. It is stated that the arguments he used were so cogent, that the royal pair were on the point of consenting, when Torquemada rushed into the royal presence with a crucifix in his hand, and thrusting it before the sovereigns, exclaimed: ''Judas Iscariot sold his master for thirty pieces of silver; you wish to sell him for 300,000 ducats; here he is, take him and sell him.'' This concluded the argument; the fate of the Spanish Jews was now irrevocably sealed. In proportion as the day of their departure drew near, and the means of realisation became more difficult, their anxiety to dispose of their worldly goods grew greater; valuable plots of land were sold for a few pieces of cloth, fine houses were exchanged for a couple of mules, and in many cases the riches of the Israelites melted away into those few articles, which they could carry with them, and the beasts, which were to transport them. Moreover, the convents and public institutions, the nobles, and persons of every class, were largely indebted to the Jews, and as no provision was made for the collection of the debts becoming due to them after the date of their enforced departure, their losses from this source were almost incalculable, and the pain to the debtors was of course proportionately enormous. Despite the edict, saddles and furniture were stuffed full of gold pieces, while such as could succeed in transmuting their money into bills of exchange, which were not then very general in Spain, did so on any terms, however ruinous.

Sad and harrowing were the scenes presented in these last days of sojourn in Spain. In most communities visits were paid by the Jews to the tombs of their ancestors, to which they bade a long farewell. In Plasencia the Jews made over to the city their cemetery and a considerable tract of adjoining land, under condition that their burial-ground should never be built over; in Vitoria a similar compact was arranged, and in Segovia amid tears and lamentations they removed many of the tomb-stones of their fathers, and carried them with them in their long wanderings. During the whole of that sad month of July were to be seen, along the high-roads of Spain, the long files of the Hebrew people, downcast and sorrowful, some in the decrepitude of age, others in the tenderness of youth, the sick, and the halt, the infirm and the weak, included in the common fate. The outcasts wended their weary way under a scorching sun, toiling over the arid, dusty plains, and the rugged mountains, and through the

rocky defiles which characterise the Peninsula, con-
veying with them the scrolls of their holy law, and
the few remnants of their wrecked fortunes, and
frequently casting a lingering look back towards
those dear homes which they were never to see
again. The mocking gestures of the peasantry and
townsmen, as they passed along, the contempt and
scorn which they met with on every side, made these
melancholy processions still more painful, and at
length by the first days of August the exodus was
completed, and the doom was fulfilled. By a strange
coincidence the 2nd of August 1492 fell upon the
9th Ab, 5252, A.M., and this anniversary of the
destruction of the first and of the second temples,
and of so many troubles to the House of Israel, had
never recurred before with such sad reality as on
the present occasion. The number of Jews who thus
quitted Spain has never been ascertained; Mariana
puts it as high as 800,000, whilst some other his-
torians estimate it as low as 160,000; so that taking
a middle course we may probably assume it to have
been little short of 400,000.

The fate of the exiles was varied in the different
lands where they sought refuge. Those who escaped
to Morocco and Algiers found an inhospitable reception; many were sold into slavery, some starved
to death, whilst others were ripped open in the
hopes of finding gold pieces in their bodies, and a
few preferred to return to Spain and receive baptism,
a fate which was forced on some others, who were
wrecked on the Spanish coast. In Turkey they were

well received, and Sultan Bajazet is said to have remarked: "A politic king, indeed, must be this Don Fernando, who impoverishes his kingdom to enrich our own." In Italy, though Genoa would only allow them to remain three days, they found in most states permission to abide, and in some, as in Naples, they received a hearty welcome; into Navarre some few were admitted, but only to await in a couple of years an entire expulsion with the rest of their brethren. The major part emigrated to Portugal, the aged and noble Rabbi, and great Talmudist, Isaac Aboab of Toledo, having obtained, despite much opposition, the permission of King John II. to their entering the country, though only in consideration of each immigrant paying a capitation-tax, and on the understanding that within eight months they should leave the country, for which purpose proper ships should be provided by the government at moderate rates of passage-money. Indeed, it appears that the Portuguese Jews themselves were alarmed at this enormous immigration of their brethren. Their own position was at this period by no means assured, and so sudden an increase of their number, composed of persons mostly in distressed circumstances, was naturally calculated to create the most anxious misgivings. Nevertheless, it is stated (though there are great discrepancies as to numbers), that nearly 150,000 of those expelled from Spain availed themselves of this temporary refuge.

A remarkable fact connected with this expulsion was the firm attitude of the Rabbis, who everywhere counselled steadfastness and resignation; people bowed down by suffering passively submitted to their doom, and thus, though some few Jews, and among them Abraham Senior and his son, preferred conversion to banishment, the total number who rather submitted to baptism than to exile was quite insignificant. The fires and terrors of the Inquisition had already sufficiently proved that conversion afforded but slight guarantee for safety, and that New Christians were but little more free from persecution than had been those who had not abandoned the faith of their fathers.

Thus was Spain deprived of her large Jewish population; the synagogues were purified and used as Christian churches; the vast sums of money which were owed to the Jews, and the still larger amounts which they were forced to leave behind them, found their way partly into the hands of their debtors, or still more into those of the sovereign; the chief professors of medicine were sent out of the country, to the terrible inconvenience of the population, and trade and industry languished till they almost died out.

Unfortunately at the time of the expulsion the plague was raging in Castile, and the fugitives brought with them the disease, propagating it wherever they went, and not unnaturally causing their advent to be viewed with loathing and horror. This circumstance induced King John to hasten their departure from Portugal, for which purpose ships were duly provided according to the agreement, but such was the temper of the captains and sailors, that they subjected the Jews to the hardest possible conditions; they plundered them of their goods and valuables even to their very clothes, and landed them naked and bare of everything on barren points of the African coast, leaving them to die of starvation or to be sold into slavery to the Moors. Nor was this all: the King wrested from their parents all children between the ages of three and ten of those Jewish immigrants who from poverty or otherwise had omitted to pay the capitation-tax on entering, or who were forced to remain in Portugal, and had them transported to the newly discovered Islands of St. Thomas, which then swarmed with alligators and other beasts of prey, to be brought up as Christians. Six hundred of the richest families of the Spanish Jews, however, had by a separate transaction procured for themselves the right of remaining in Portugal, on payment of 60,000 gold cousados, and a few useful mechanics were also exempted from the action of the general decree.

These painful proceedings on the part of the King of Portugal lead us to consider the state of the indigenous Jewish population in that country. We have seen the high position which they had occupied for many centuries; how they had held charge of the greatest trust; how they had farmed the revenues of both Church and State, in the exercise of which office, though bringing on themselves the animadversion of the populace, they had been found to be more liberal than Christian collectors, and how until 1449 few or no attempts at persecution had been made. As has been related, Alfonso V., who reigned from 1438 to 1481, and who was principally engaged in his African campaigns, employed many Jews in places of high trust, and was generally favourable to them. It is true that during the latter part of this reign, and in the succeeding one, jealousy and bigotry were steadily growing, that edicts had been passed confining the Jews more severely to their own quarters, prohibiting them from having Christian servants, from wearing silk or jewels, or using plate, or riding on horses, edicts which must have been especially galling to persons used to a splendid mode of life, and fond to excess of display, but for all this, they were tolerated. Their worship and observances were recognised by the law, and beyond the privileges largely conceded to converts, one of which, highly immoral in its tendency, was, that any child of Jewish parents, who became a Christian in their lifetime, was to take immediate inheritance, as though the parents were already dead, their religion was not interfered with.

Alfonso's successor, John II., notwithstanding his barbarous treatment of the unfortunate Jewish fugitives from Spain, firmly resisted the introduction of the Inquisition, neither was he disposed to expel a population, whose wealth and intelligence were eminently useful; but the horrible cruelties he had perpetrated, and the persecuting spirit he had displayed, could not fail to have a fearful influence on the minds of the people in regard to the native Jews of Portugal. The bitterness of feeling which had been growing for many generations was gathering to a climax, when in 1495 Don John died, and his only legitimate son, Don Alfonso, having been killed by a fall from his horse four years before, his cousin, Don Manoel, ascended the throne.

This prince, whose success in his various enterprises and discoveries won for him the appellation of the ''Fortunate,'' commenced his reign by evincing the most tolerant spirit. He revoked the oppressive edicts of his predecessor, and restored the Jews to the position they had held before, trusting rather to obtain their conversion by mildness and mercy, than by harshness and compulsion. The Hebrews sought to show their gratitude by the offer of a large sum of money, which the King refused to accept. A learned astronomer, who in those days passed also for an astrologer, by name Abraham Çacuto, was consulted by Don Manoel on every great occasion, and other learned Jews enjoyed his protection and support. This was however but a transient gleam of sunshine, and the storm soon gathered more darkly than before. Don Manoel had hardly been a year on the throne when he sought the hand of Donna Isabella, the young widow of the late crown-prince Alfonso, and the eldest daughter of Ferdinand and Isabella. Whether he was smitten by the charms of the princess, or whether the alliance with her opened out to his ambition the vista of the eventual union of the two crowns of Spain and Portugal on his own head, and on that of his progeny, the

Catholic sovereigns having but one son, has never been proved, but certain it is, he was excessively ardent in his suit.

The princess inheriting to a marked degree the bigotry of her parents, absolutely refused to listen to the addresses of Don Manoel, unless that prince consented to banish from his dominions all Mohammedans and Jews. With regard to the former, of whom no very large number still remained in Portugal, it was agreed that their forced conversion would lead to reprisals on the many Christians who were scattered through Moslem States, and therefore it was decided to limit their penalties to expulsion, every facility being granted for their leaving the country; whilst the Jews, who had no means whatever of recrimination, were to be dealt with according to the pleasure of the sovereign. It was for many months debated whether the elimination of so large a number of the wealthiest and most industrious of the population could be effected without causing a national misfortune, and on the other hand the more moderate among the clergy submitted that baptism received under compulsion possessed no power of salvation, and was therefore inoperative; but the King was deaf to all these arguments. In December, 1496, Don Manoel issued a proclamation ordering that all non-converted Jews should leave Portugal within ten months under pain of confiscation of property, which was to fall to those who informed against all such as should disobey. Those who agreed to depart were to have powers afforded them of collecting their debts, and realising their property; they were also to have means of transport duly provided. But this was not all; in the following April appeared another edict ordaining that all the children under fourteen of those who had chosen exile rather than conversion, should be forcibly taken from their parents, and being distributed through the whole country, should be handed over to persons, who should bring them up in the Christian faith. This barbarous edict was to be carried out at the approaching Feast of Passover, which all Jews celebrate together in family groups.

The state of desperation and agony into which the Jews were plunged is hardly to be imagined. Multitudes of children were hidden away by their parents, and many were concealed by the more merciful among the Christians, but all these were diligently sought out, dragged forth, and forced to the font, while many instances occurred in which maddened fathers and mothers first destroyed their offspring with their own hands, and then committed suicide.

During the few months which remained to them, the Jews tried every means in their power to soften the heart of the King, and lastly finding all efforts without avail, they sought to be allowed three points from which they might make their exit, instead of the one sole port, which had been allotted. After dallying with them for some time, Don Manoel informed them that only one place of departure could be assigned, and that was Lisbon itself. More than 20,000 Jews under these circumstances assembled in the capital, and were lodged in a vast barrack called the Estáos, where every means of fair promise and foul intimidation was employed to make them re· nounce their faith. A fresh edict now went forth that all children between fourteen and twenty should also be taken from their parents and baptized, and multitudes were dragged forcibly by their hair and by their arms into the churches, and compelled to receive the waters of baptism, together with new names, being afterwards given over to those who undertook to instruct them in the Catholic faith. Next the parents themselves were seized, and were offered to have their children restored to them, if they would consent to be converted; in case of their refusal they were to be placed in confinement for three days without food or drink. It is indeed wonderful that any mortals could be proof against so terrible and fiendish an ordeal; yet to the glory of the Hebrew race very many still remained un-moved. Resistance was, however, not to be tolerated, and it was therefore decreed that the same fate was to be meted out to the adults and to the aged, as had already been the portion of the younger members of the race of Israel. Amid the most heart-rending cries and the most determined resistance, men and women in the flower of their days, or the decrepitude of age, were dragged into the churches, and forcibly baptized amid the mocking and exultation of an excited populace. But seven or eight of the whole number of those who maintained their constancy, succeeded in eluding force, and managed to secure a passage to the coast of Africa.

The Jews who were still scattered through other parts of the country, seeing the fate of their brethren, were forced to assume the garb of Christianity, many seeking in a self-inflicted death the only refuge from apostasy, and thus, nominally, was Judaism extinguished in Portugal, as it had been five years before in Spain.

Amid these horrors and barbarities were celebrated the nuptials of Don Manoel and Donna Isabel, but the union was of short duration; the princess died in little more than a year, following to the tomb her brother Don John, the only son of Ferdinand and Isabella, and later on the King married her sister Donna Maria. The wily monarch, who by such absolute and ruthless acts had complied with the conditions of the princess and her bigoted parents, and had thus managed ostensibly to purge the land from Judaism and Mohammedanism without conceding the establishment of the Inquisition, despite all the powerful interest which had been brought to bear upon him to that end, now sought by outward acts of conciliation and mildness to reconcile the New Christians to the religion they had been forced to adopt. Later in the year 1497 appeared an edict by which the converts from Judaism were shielded from persecution for the next twenty years, during which time every means was to be provided for instructing them in their new faith. At the end of this period all difference between Old and New Christians was to cease. Those then accursed of Jewish practices were to be handed over to the civil law, and if found guilty were to be punished with the confiscation of their property, which was to fall to the next Christian heir. The population, however, was not to be satisfied with this mild treatment of the Hebrew race, and the hatred they bore to the converts was, if possible, more deadly than that which they had manifested while they openly remained Jews. Restriction followed restriction, till the position of the New Christians became so intolerable, that large numbers sought refuge, after disposing of their worldly goods, by emigrating to other lands; but to the great majority this course was evidently impossible.

The Spanish monarchs continued to work vigorously to induce their son-in-law to allow the introduction of the Inquisition into his dominions; but all they could obtain was a law which prohibited any Spaniard from fixing his residence in Portugal, unless he could show that he had not been guilty of any offence against religion. This law, however, was quite inoperative, and numbers of New Christians from Spain, terrified by the proceedings of the Inquisition, still continued to cross the frontier, adding thereby to the popular outcry. In 1503 a famine, and in 1504 a riot in the streets of Lisbon, gave rise to outbursts of the rage of the populace, and in 1506 the plague further worked up the feelings of the multitude. On Whitsunday of this year, whilst the congregation were supplicating for a deliverance from the scourge in one of the principal churches, the reflection of light from a crystal covering the Host above a crucifix caused the excited populace to cry out "A miracle, a miracle!" The effulgence was evidently but the play of light, and one of those present, unfortunately a New Christian, was heard to observe that he could see nothing remarkable in the appearance.

Those near him, hearing the observation, rushed on the unfortunate man, killing him on the spot, and burning his body on a pile heaped up in a moment in the public square. Soon the whole city was in an uproar, and the air was rent with cries of "Heresy, heresy!" The populace seized hold of all the New Christians they could find, indiscriminately slaying among the number many old Christians, who were thought to have Jewish features, destroyed and pillaged houses, and gave over the capital to scenes of havoc and destruction. Men, women, and children were dragged from the churches, where many had sought refuge, and burnt alive in the public streets, and it was only at the end of the third day, when more than 3,000 persons had been sacrificed to the popular fury, that the tardy intervention of the law managed to secure a semblance of order.

Don Manoel, incensed at these rabid persecutions, sought to reassure the New Christians by a fresh edict, by which he granted them full equality before the law, and extended their term for thoroughly instructing themselves in the tenets of the Christian faith till the year 1526. It was furthermore ordained that all New Christians were at liberty to leave the country if they pleased, whilst those who had already quitted, were assured that they would be unmolested if they chose to return.

During the remainder of this reign, which closed in 1521, it does not appear that the converts suffered any violent persecution, though the feeling towards them but little improved. The new King, John III. (1521-1557), was possessed with the most intense hatred of the Jewish race; nevertheless, urged by the ministers of his father, he began his reign with a semblance of toleration, and promised the New Christians a prolongation of their time of sufferance till 1534.

And now recommenced in earnest the intrigues for the establishment of the Inquisition in Portugal. A converted Jew, named Henriquez Nunez, surnamed, from his orthodox Catholic practices, "Firma-fé," wormed himself into the confidence of his former brethren in faith, and making use of the secrets thus treacherously obtained, conveyed to the King the alarming fact that the greater part of the New Christians were still entirely Jews at heart, and bore but the outward semblance of their adopted faith. He therefore strongly urged the institution of the Tribunal, which in Spain had proved so eminently useful in detecting and eradicating heresy. This man was stabbed to death in 1524,—a deed which was visited with terrible consequences on the New Christians. Neither the Pope nor the Portuguese clergy, nor even the mass of the people, viewed

with much satisfaction the institution of the Inquisition; but the Queen, a sister of Charles V., that
powerful monarch himself, and the Dominican
monks, were untiring in their efforts, and in December, 1531, Clement VII. issued a Bull for the
establishment of the Tribunal in Portugal. For ten
years, however, the matter was kept pending; the
New Christians were naturally horror-stricken, and
vast sums of Jewish gold found their way to the
treasury of St. Peter, to endeavour to avert the
threatened doom. Among other means they maintained a secret envoy at Rome, a converted Jew
named Duarte da Paz, high in the confidence of the
King; but in 1539 this man, who only worked for
his personal interests, found it to his advantage to
denounce the proceedings of the New Christians to
Don John. It happened, however, that Duarte had
incurred the suspicion of the Pope; he was thrown
into prison, and on his liberation he fled into Turkey,
and there died as a Mohammedan.

Many were the plots and counter-plots, the Bulls
and Counter-Bulls, till at last, in 1541, the Court of
the Inquisition began its terrible career in Lisbon,
and the first *auto-da-fé* was celebrated there in
October of that year. One final effort was made in
1519 by the Jews to procure their readmission into
Spain, when on the accession of Charles V. (First, of
Spain) to the throne, an important deputation of
Marannos waited upon him in Flanders, and offered
the sum of 800,000 gold ducats, provided he would
grant them permission to return, with the free exer-

¶ Que os Iudeus tragam gorra, ou barrete amarelo

OM PHILIPPE per graça de Deos Rey de Portugal, & dos Algarues, daquem & dalem mar em Africa, senhor de Guine, da conquista, nauegação, comercio de Ethiopia, Arabia, Persia, & da India, &c. Faço saber que o senhor Rey dom Manoel meu auo que Deos tem, no anno da era de nosso Senhor Iesu Christo, de mil & quatrocentos & nouenta & sete fez húa ley per que mandou que todos os Iudeus que andassem em seus Reinos de Portugal se saissem delles é certo termo que lhes afsinou sobpena de morte natural & de perdimento de suas fazendas pera quem os accusasse, pelas razões na dita ley declaradas. E depois elRey dom Ioam meu senhor que Deos tem no anno de mil & quinhentos trinta & sete, ordenou que os Iudeus que andassem nos ditos Reinos trouxessem hum sinal pera seré conhecidos, & que fosse húa estrela de pano vermelho de seis pernas, que trariá sobre o ombro direito afsi da capa como do pelote, sob as penas na dita Ordenação declaradas, como nella mais largamente se conthem. E porquanto sou informado, que os Iudeus que com minha licença vem aos ditos Reinos, & os que ora nelles andam, não trazem o dito sinal, & outros o trazem tam piqueno, & de tal maneira o encobrem, que não sam conhecidos por Iudeus, nem se consegue o effeito da dita ley. Querendo em ello prouer, ey por bem & mando, que daqui em diante todo o Iudeu que aos ditos meus Reinos de Portugal vier, tanto que nelles entrar, traga hua gorra, ou barrete, ou sombreiro amarelo na cabeça, a qual gorra, ou barrete, ou sombreiro, não trara cuberto com outra cousa, sobpena que sendo achado sem a dita gorra, ou barrete, ou sombreiro descuberto, seja publicaméte açoutado, & pague cem cruzados ametade pera os cattuos, & a outra ametade pera qué o acusar, & seja

FIRST PAGE FROM PHILIP II'S DECREE, MADRID, 1583 (IN PORTUGUESE), ORDERING ALL JEWS ARRIVING OR STAYING IN PORTUGAL TO WEAR YELLOW HATS

cise of their religion. The monarch, who was at the time hardly pressed for money, showed every sign of yielding, but Cardinal Ximenes, who after the death of Deza, the successor of Torquemada, had become Inquisitor-General, despatched an envoy to Brussels, begging the Emperor to desist from a transaction by which the interests of the faith were to be bartered away for vile lucre.

Thus in the middle of the sixteenth century, the golden age of modern art, the flourishing period of newly-revived literature, when the rough habits, engendered by constant turmoil and discord were giving place to milder manners, the awful spectre of the Inquisition became a living reality in the whole breadth of the Peninsula, and throughout those enormous colonies in America, in Africa, and in Asia, which were subject to the crowns of Spain and Portugal. There is little doubt that the recent birth of Protestantism, which threatened to overwhelm the whole of Roman Catholic Christendom, and which gave so vast an amount of trouble to the Emperor Charles V. in his German and Flemish dominions, strengthened the hold of the Inquisition in Spain, and operated largely in procuring its establishment in Portugal. As, however, the new doctrines found but little favour in either country, the weight of its terrors fell principally on the Jews, its machinery being also often artfully adapted, so as to draw within its meshes all individuals who were in any degree deemed by the Holy Court to be obnoxious,

but whose position rendered them difficult to deal
with by any other process.

Even cardinals and bishops, and the princes and
princesses of the royal house, did not escape without
incurring the censure of the Tribunal, and the unfortunate Don Carlos, Philip II.'s only son then
living, was probably a victim to its machinations.
Prominent political personages and ministers of
state were particularly amenable to the suspicion of
the Inquisition, and all those in authority, whom it
in any way desired to remove, were sure to fall into
its grasp, and to be crushed within its fearful fangs.
Thus it became a gigantic engine no less politically
than socially, and assuming to control the religious
life of men, grew to be in reality the most vital, or
rather the most deadly organ of the State.   The
press too was subjected to the control of the holy
office, and thus through the aid of the strictest cen-
sorship it stifled scientific investigation and original
thought, and made itself master of every avenue of
the human mind.   The system of delation and secret
information was so subtle and so widely spread, that
no person, whatever might be his condition, or however orthodox might be his practice, was free from
incurring suspicion.   The most elaborate method of
espionage was devised, children were encouraged to
reveal the private practices of their parents, servants
were invited to divulge the secrets of the closet,
workmen were enticed to denounce the procedure of
their employers, and the domesticity of the family
was   unveiled   by   every   possible   artifice.   Thus

mutual confidence between man and man was closed up; reticence and deception took the place of brotherly intercourse and good fellowship, and a sullen reserve begotten by suspicion and fear reigned through the whole of society, and in time assumed the form of a national characteristic.

In order to extend the working of the Tribunal over as wide a field as possible, anonymous declarations were accepted as valid, and many were induced to betray others in the hope of thereby avoiding suspicion for themselves, while private enmity and malice found no easier manner of gratification than by handing over the enemy to the tender mercies of the Holy Court. The suspected were seized without notice, and dragged, often from their beds, from the family circle, to be lodged in the dungeons of the Inquisition. Family and friends were neither allowed to know the charges preferred against the prisoner, nor to hold any communication with him, and thus wives frequently found themselves in a moment condemned to widowhood, and children to orphanage, without knowing the fate of the dear one so ruthlessly snatched from their embrace. Long years of anxiety and watchfulness, of painful expectation and wearing uncertainty, tediously passed away, and when such prisoners as obtained a pardon came forth, and were restored to their families, their sickened forms and emaciated frames long betokened the treatment to which they had been subjected. Moreover, through the remainder of their lives they were ever afterwards zealously watched, as a "relapse" was never forgiven.

The course of legal procedure was arranged in such a manner as to leave it entirely in the power of the judges to establish the guilt or innocence of the accused. Prisoners were to be "admonished" on each of the first three days of their imprisonment, and in urging them to confess, the Inquisition lost no opportunity of asserting that voluntary penitents would be mildly dealt with. As the accused were never informed who were the parties who denounced them, or what formed the leading points of accusation, it was rare that confessions either of innocence or guilt proved satisfactory to the judges. If at the end of these admonitions and examinations no satisfactory result could be arrived at, a paper compiled by the Inquisitors, and setting forth the nature of the accusations, together with a number of other crimes, of which the prisoner had never been really accused, was handed to him, and an advocate from among the legal officers of the court was, if desired, placed at his disposal. As, however, the accused could only communicate with his counsel in the presence of the Inquisitors and the registrar, this advantage proved entirely nugatory, and the prisoner was remanded and committed anew to his cell, either for a future interrogation, which might be delayed for weeks, months, or, even as was often the case, for years, or else in order to be dragged forth again to submit to torture, by which means it was hoped to bring forth more satisfactory confessions. To

A SANBENITO
(After Picart.)

such as yielded readily to the admonitions of the Inquisitors, and, admitting the truth of the accusations against them, promised amendment for the future, absolution was generally accorded, on condition of performing penance.

This was of various degrees, according to the offence, involving a longer or lesser term of imprisonment, at the end of which the absolved were led forth from the dungeons clad in the sanbenito, in which they were bound to stand at the doors of certain churches, and exposed to the revilings of the multitude. This process had to be repeated during a given period, and sometimes for life, from Sunday to Sunday, and on various festivals, and from time to time they had to listen to sermons in which the wickedness of their acts was portrayed in lively colours, and every exhortation to repentance was rehearsed.

The loss of their property was entailed on such as were more deeply dyed with infidelity, while to those who were more easily absolved a total or partial restitution was conceded; but the administration of the officials who were appointed to take charge of the effects of prisoners, while undergoing trial, was generally found to have ruined the estates, and the less wealthy equally experienced that their various industries had suffered, or had actually died out. Thus the pardoned were returned to the world, beggared in means of existence, and branded for ever with the mark of heresy and infamy; moreover, the withering glance of the Inquisition, like the "evil

eye'' of oriental superstition, was in future always
directed towards them, and tales of relapse were easily
invented and fastened on to those who had once owned
themselves guilty of the crime of having wavered in
their belief.

The tribunals of the Inquisition were as a rule
installed in stately, though generally gloomy, palaces,
where the Inquisitors, their secretaries, registrars,
and familiars were lodged in a becoming manner.
These buildings contained audience-chambers, halls
for the examination of prisoners and witnesses (who
were never allowed to be confronted together), and
also the prisons, which were of three kinds: the first
were denominated ''public,'' and were intended for
such as, not having been guilty directly of crimes of
faith, were yet deemed legally amenable to the Inquisition; the second were called ''intermediary,''
and were reserved for such officers of the Holy Court
as had misconducted themselves; and the third were
the ''secret'' cells, which formed the great bulk, being
reserved for those who were accused of breaches of
faith, and who had been condemned to incarceration
for a term or for life.

These secret prisons were generally in the base-
ment of the building, deep below the soil, dimly
lighted, hardly ventilated, and reeking with filth,
which was but rarely removed; sometimes the prisoner was solitary, sometimes four or five persons were
thrust into the same narrow cell, about eight feet by
six in size, where the fetid atmosphere, intense heat,
and close confinement frequently generated fevers.

Moreover, the food afforded to these unfortunate captives was of the coarsest and most unwholesome description; hard and mouldy bread and impure water, of which one jar only a week was supplied for all purposes, formed the staple of their diet, and when on rare occasions more generous food was allowed, it was frequently tainted, and hardly ever really nourishing.

Thus lodged and thus fed the prisoner might languish, neglected and forgotten, year after year, and many were the instances in which a prolonged incarceration, under these painful circumstances, finished by depriving the captive of his reason, leaving him to end his days in the condition of a brute. It was a frequent practice, when prisoners were awaiting further interrogation, to send persons into their cells under pretence of affording them consolation, but in reality to entice them into conversation, and thus to worm out, by means of unguarded expressions, proofs which might lead to their condemnation. Far away, in the remotest part of the building, was the subterranean chamber where torture was administered—a large bare vault, dimly lighted by lamps, and whose whole furniture consisted of a crucifix hung on the wall, and the grim apparatus of agony, under which the victim was to writhe. It is neither profitable, nor desirable to dwell on the various modes of torture which the demoniacal ingenuity of one portion of our species has invented, in order to inflict suffering and agony on another.

In various times and countries we hear of the

rack and the wheel, of thumb-screws, iron boots, collars and girdles of inverted nails, metal stools under which a slow fire was kindled, and similar atrocious engines, and as we gaze at these rusty emblems of infernal cruelty in various museums and collections, we shudder to think that men with minds similar to our own could have devised such horrors.

It is, however, proper to enumerate three special modes of torture, which were, it is said, devised by the Inquisition, and were certainly generally employed by it in addition to those instruments we have mentioned above. One was that by which the prisoner was drawn up by the hands by means of a pulley, cords being tied around his wrists, and heavy weights attached to his feet; when near the ceiling he was suddenly allowed to drop to within a few feet of the floor, by which awful shock his limbs were dislocated. This process was often repeated two or three times on the same individual. Another was the placing of the prisoner in a horizontal position, the middle of the body being slightly elevated above the extremities, and resting on an iron bar, and the head and feet being made fast by passing tight ropes round them; while thus held his nostrils were stopped, and his open mouth covered with a cloth, on which water was allowed to fall from a height, till it almost forced the cloth down his throat, when it was pulled out again, so as to allow the respiration to return, and then the same proceeding was gone through over again. The third mode of torture was the strapping of the prisoner on the ground with his

Various Manners of Torturing during the Inquisition.
(After Picart.)

feet, which had been greased with lard, turned towards a roasting fire, in which position of agony he might be kept for an hour.

These tortures were administered by "familiars" dressed in black, wearing mantles which covered their faces, holes being left for the eyes and mouth. Two Inquisitors were present to conduct the interrogation, and to take down the deposition of the accused. As may readily be supposed, very few could maintain their composure or their constancy under such terrible inflictions; maddened with agony the sufferers confessed to the most improbable frequently impossible crimes, generally implicating by their incoherent statements as well friends and relations as many other persons whom they hardly knew. The next day, or as soon as the prisoner was sufficiently recovered, a copy of his confession was presented to him for ratification, and notwithstanding the falsity or absurdity of its various points, such was the fear of a repetition, or as it was called, "continuation" of the torture, that it rarely happened that the prisoner failed to confirm his depositions. In those instances, where the accused recanted, the further application of torture was, as a rule, successful in wresting from him a full confirmation of all the previous statements, and usually much additional matter. In fact, courage and constancy availed nothing, as, in the parlance of the Inquisitors, these virtues were qualified as obduracy and impenitence, and those who displayed them were rewarded by being immured for years or for life in horrible dungeons, or were handed over to the secular arm, an euphemistic expression, which signified that the victims were to be sentenced to perish in the fires of an *auto-da-fé,* the Holy Court being too merciful itself to pronounce a sentence of death.

It is hardly remarkable that with so elaborate a process to criminate the accused, and with so little facility for establishing innocence, the instances of complete acquittal were so rare as hardly ever to occur, and it is reckoned that far less than one prisoner in a thousand left the walls of the Inquisition entirely unscathed, so that it became a proverb, "A man may leave the Inquisition without being burned, but he is sure to be singed."

Those condemned to form part of an *auto-da-fé* were kept imprisoned often for many years, till some grand festival, such as a coronation or a royal marriage, gave occasion for public rejoicing, when the grim spectacle was exhibited to the multitude of the faithful. An attempt must be made to describe this proceeding in order to give an idea of its full meaning. About a month before the date appointed, generally on a high festival, the announcement was made that an *auto-da-fé* was fixed for a given date. The proclamation was made in grand state by the Inquisitor-General with his numerous staff, his proud standard of scarlet and gold floating before him, and amid an array of troops in gay uniforms, and of priests and monks in varied habits, with heralds accompanied by a long procession of saints, images, relics, and crucifixes glittering with precious stones, parading

the city amid cries of ''Viva la fé!'' ''the faith for
ever!'' The interval between the proclamation and
the execution was occupied in erecting, in the principal square or Plaza Mayor, the vast theatre for the
spectators and performers in the grand ''Fiesta,'' as
it was called.

One of the most remarkable of these shows took
place in Madrid on Sunday, June 30, 1680, on the
occasion of the marriage of the almost demented
King, Charles II., then about twenty years of age,
with the Princess Marie Louise of Orleans, niece of
Louis XIV., the account of which, gathered from
various sources, by Kayserling and others, it may be
interesting to follow. An ampitheatre had been
constructed on the Plaza Mayor, with the box for the
King, Queen, and royal family on the one side, and
on the other a raised daïs for the Inquisitor-General,
his superior officers, and the higher clergy. The
ministers and Court officials in gala uniforms, and
the various trade corporations in state dresses, with
a motley group of monks in their respective habits,
together with an overwhelming multitude of the
populace, all assembled in the imposing arena, amid
the pealing of bells and the chaunts of priests.

The ceremony began about six in the morning,
and by eight, the King, Queen, Queen-mother, and
Court, the foreign ambassadors with numberless
ladies in Court dresses, and the innumerable digni-
taries of the State, had taken the places reserved for
them opposite the gallery of the Inquisitors, before
which floated the green cross, the banner of the

Holy Office. The cry "Viva la fé!" burst forth from myriads of throats, as the melancholy procession was seen entering the arena. A hundred charcoal-burners, clad in black, and armed with pikes and helmets, came first, as was their prescriptive right, they having furnished the wood for the sacrifice; then followed a number of Dominican monks, and the Duke of Medina Celi, hereditary standard-bearer of the Inquisitors, with other friars and nobles bearing banners and crosses. Thirty-four images of life size, with their names inscribed in large letters, and borne by the familiars of the Inquisitors, repre-sented those who had died in prison, or escaped by flight; Dominican friars with coffins came next, bearing the bones of those who had been convicted of heresy after death, and then appeared fifty-four men and women holding lighted tapers, and clad in the sanbenito and coroza, or high cap, almost all of whom had been convicted of Judaising, but had confessed and repented. Lastly followed eighteen Jews and Jewesses, mostly persons of humble rank, also wearing the sanbenito and coroza, who were to bear witness in the flames to their steadfastness to the law of Israel. Most of them, haggard and worn by long imprisonment, seemed languid and indifferent, quite resigned to quit the world in which they had suffered so intensely, but one beautiful girl about seventeen, as she approached the royal stand, called out, "Noble queen, cannot your royal presence save me from this? I sucked in my religion with my mother's milk; must I now die for it?"

In the Plaza
(After a

adrid 1680
Rici).

The young Queen's eyes filled with tears; she hid her face, and the sad procession passed on. High Mass was then celebrated before a grand altar, which had been erected for the purpose, with all the pomp which was thought befitting to the occasion. At noon the Inquisitor-General with a staff of his officials passed over to the King, with the Gospels in his hands, upon which he administered to Charles the oath that he would support the faith and the Inquisition, and do all that lay in him to extirpate heresy. Next followed a sermon from one of the principal chaplains of the King, Fray Tomas Navarro. The text of this lengthy lecture which lasted a couple of hours was, ''Arise, O Lord, and judge thy cause,'' and this was the refrain of the whole composition, which from beginning to end was one vast tissue of abuse of the Hebrew people, and one long string of curses supported by passages from Scripture violently wrested from their context. He adjured the Jews before him to acknowledge the wickedness of their ways, and to accept the doctrines of salvation before that last moment of life, which was so painfully drawing near. After this the prisoners were brought to the staging, which had been erected in the middle of the arena; each entered a sort of cage, and the name of the individual, with the nature of the crimes of which he or she was convicted, was read out in a loud voice. The day was unusually sultry, but the King sat out the fourteen hours without so much as moving to take a mouthful of food.

Monks were continually hovering round the un-

fortunate Jews urging them to repent, and to acknowledge their abominable heresy, but all in vain: the
harder the trial to which they were subjected, the
higher rose the heroism of these Hebrew men and
women, who were thus barbarously exposed like wild
beasts in the arena, when separated by but a few
hours from the most painful death. At length the
long-delayed shadows of this summer's eve drew on,
the evening Angelus pealed forth in its impressive
tones, vespers were grandly chaunted, absolution was
pronounced, and the Inquisitor leaving his throne
passed over to the King, when the fictitious ceremony
took place of handing over the prisoners to the secular
power, since the Church could not pronounce a ver-
dict of death. Then in the growing darkness was
organised the horrible procession to the Puerta
de Fuencarral, outside which was the Quemadero,
where the final scene was to take place. Those who
at the last moment confessed their penitence, had
the grace conceded to them of being strangled at the
foot of the pile; the bodies of such, the bones of the
dead heretics, and the effigies of the absent were
first deposited at the stake, and lastly the living
victims, men and women, mounted the pile with so
firm a step that the chroniclers were fain to ascribe
their courage to some diabolical charm, in order not
to be forced to own their admiration. The King
himself kindled with his own hand the fatal pile, and
soon the flames in which these noble beings perished
mounted towards heaven amid the deafening plaudits
of the multitude, and the whole city was lit up by

the lurid light, which represented so vividly, as it was meant to represent, the flames of hell.

Those so-called penitents, who had life spared to live a life-long torment, were forced to assist at the horrible spectacle, after which they were taken back to their dungeons, which many of them were never to leave again, whilst others in a few days were sent off to the galleys.

Such were the scenes which with more or less similar circumstances were enacted in every large city in Spain, and Portugal, and in all the immense colonies, and dependencies of the two crowns. Sometimes twice or thrice in a year, sometimes not for several years, together, depending much on the personal character of the sovereign, and still more on the greater or less degree of severity, which marked the Inquisitor-General. The monarchs of the Bourbon dynasty refused to be present at any *auto-da-fé,* and though one was celebrated on the accession of Philip V., in 1701, the King could not be persuaded to witness it; from this time the exhibition grew less frequent, and the last occasion on which a human being was burned alive in the name of the faith was at Seville in 1781, and the victim then was not a member of the Hebrew race.

In Portugal these human sacrifices did not survive so long, and although a grand *auto-da-fé* was celebrated in Lisbon in 1705, on which occasion the Archbishop of Cranganor delivered the voluminous and vituperative sermon, to which David Nieto, Chief Rabbi of the Jews in London, afterwards pub-

lished a reply, the close of this long series of tragedies was not far distant. This took place in October,
1739; the last sacrifice was an illustrious one,
namely, Antonio José da Silva, a dramatic author of
much merit, who was born in Brazil, to which country, taken from the Portuguese by the Dutch, and
afterwards restored to the former, large numbers of
converted Jews had flocked, and had there resumed
their faith.

Antonio had been brought by his father, with the
rest of his family, to settle in Lisbon; but it was
not long before both father and son incurred the suspicion of the Inquisition, from the censures of which,
however, they contrived to purge themselves. Da
Silva henceforward led a secluded and literary life,
enjoying the society of his young wife, and blessed
with a little daughter, whose second birthday he was
celebrating, when the familiars of the Holy Office
pounced in upon the family circle, and hurried off
him and his wife and mother to the dungeons of the
Inquisition, upon the deposition of a negro maid-
servant. After two years of painful confinement,
and despite great interest exerted on his behalf, the
young author was condemned to the flames, his wife
and mother being sentenced to imprisonment as
penitents, the latter surviving her son's sacrifice but
three days.[1]

[1] The terrible earthquake of Lisbon, which happened on November 1st, 1755, and laid the greater part of the city in ruins,
spreading death and desolation everywhere, and destroying between 30,000 and 40,000 of the inhabitants, proved the means

As may easily be imagined, many of the New Christians who still remained attached to Judaism sought, where possible, to effect their escape from Spain and Portugal to happier countries. Those who from force of circumstances, or from worldly considerations, remained behind, endeavoured by a public profession of Catholic orthodoxy, and the secret practice of Jewish ceremonies, to temporise between the loss of earthly possessions, or of life itself, and the sacrifice of every consideration, which their consciences held sacred. Many learned Jews sought refuge in the various Courts of Italy, where science and literature were specially cultivated. The distinguished family of the Usques were warmly received by the Duke of Ferrara, under whose patron-

of saving a considerable number of Jews from the jaws of the Inquisition. The palace of the Holy Court was overthrown in the common ruin, the walls of the prison house were violently split open, the gaolers fled for their lives, and such of the captives as escaped the general destruction, scared and horror-stricken, found themselves suddenly and fearfully restored to freedom. Bare of everything, and only possessed of the clothes they stood in, they lurked about among the smouldering ruins till they found, amid the general horror and consternation, a means of escape. Many of the New Christians thus freed managed to communicate with their families, and hastily collecting such valuables as were portable, and which were spared from the wreck of the earthquake, sought refuge on board the English and Dutch vessels in the harbour, meeting with a hospitable reception, and securing a passage to more tolerant lands. The Palace of the Inquisition in Lisbon seems never to have been rebuilt on the same scale as before, and its site is now occupied by the Great Theatre, in the Praza de Maria Segunda, commonly called the 'Rocio.'

age Abraham Usque published his translation of the
Bible into Spanish—a work which had become very
necessary, since the New Christians, being forced to
abandon the study of Hebrew, were gradually losing
all knowledge of the sacred language. Congregations
of Spanish Jews were planted in Florence, Venice,
and Leghorn, where their beautiful synagogue still
attests no less their devotion than their wealth. The
whole littoral of the Mediterranean, Morocco, Algiers,
Tripoli, Tunis, Egypt, Syria, and the Turkish Empire, with the many islands of the Archipelago,
became seats of Jewish industry, and to this day
the Spanish language, full of antique forms, and
written in Hebrew characters, constitutes the ver-
nacular of hundreds of thousands of the descendants of the exiles throughout the whole of these
countries.

Numbers found their way to the American colonies, whither the Inquisition followed them, so that
they were forced to settle in the various territories
and islands acquired by the Dutch and the English,
where they openly re-assumed Judaism. A vast
number established themselves in Holland, where,
after its dearly-bought independence was established,
a toleration, at first begrudged, was soon fully accorded to them. Here they founded synagogues, the
first of which was opened in Amsterdam in 1598;
here too they established charitable institutions and
schools, and here they flourished during the seven-
teenth and eighteenth centuries in a remarkable
degree. Some were allowed by Henry II. to settle

in Bordeaux, Bayonne, and other towns in the south of France, and a few wandered into Hungary and the German Empire, thus reuniting themselves with the mass of their brethren, from whom they had for so many centuries been severed, and who had from time immemorial inhabited Central Europe, forming in this manner a slender chain between the Sephardim (Spanish Jews) of the East with those of Holland and the West.

The Dutch Republic became a second Spain to them, as Spain had been a second Judæa. Here the fugitives, freed from the horrible incubus of the Inquisition, threw off the hated garb of Catholicism, assuming Hebrew names in addition to those high-sounding family appellations with which they had been endowed by the noble Spaniards, who had stood sponsors for them at the font—the Alvarezes, the de Castros, the Mendozas, the de Souzas, the Aguilars, the d'Almeidas, the de Laras, the da Silvas, &c., all recalling the noblest names of Castilian and Lusitanian chivalry. Here they at once sought to be inducted into the practices and ceremonies of the Jewish religion, which generations of disguise had almost effaced from their recollection, and here they diligently studied the Hebrew language, to which they were entirely strangers.

Numbers of authors soon appeared, and a copious flow of elegant literature, in verse and in prose, chiefly bearing on religious subjects, generally in Spanish, sometimes in Portuguese, and occasionally in Hebrew, issued from the press. The Jews of

Holland were eminently successful in pursuits of industry and commerce, by means of which large fortunes were accumulated, and important families were founded. The present splendid Portuguese synagogue of Amsterdam, bearing testimony to the importance of the congregation, was finished in 1660, four years prior to which date Manasseh ben Israel had obtained, from the Lord Protector, Cromwell, a somewhat informal permission for Jews to re-enter England, to which country many emigrated from Holland before the close of the century. Congregations were also formed in Hamburg and in Copenhagen, and the Spanish Jews, bearing with them their traditions, their industry and their wealth, together with the courtly bearing and gentle languages of the Peninsula, became diffused through all the leading centres of civilisation.

Among the many learned Jews who shone forth brilliantly amid the revived lustre of their community in Holland, one stands pre-eminent, namely, Baruch de Espinoza, better known as Benedict Spinoza, who was born in 1632, but whether in the Peninsula or in Amsterdam is not fully proved. This bold and profound philosopher, who had in early youth deeply studied the Hebrew writings, soon found the circle of Rabbinical reasoning too narrow for him, and after perfecting himself in Latin, he threw the whole force of his intellect into the rationalistic philosophy of Descartes. Boldly announcing his deistical, or rather pantheistical convictions, he entirely withdrew from the practices of Judaism, and though not

adopting any other form of religion, he became so
estranged from the Jews, to whom his philosophy
was eminently distasteful, that a public ''Herem'' or
excommunication was fulminated against him from
the synagogue in 1656. Shunned by his own people,
he pursued his studies in retirement, maintaining
himself as an optician in the suburbs of Amsterdam,
whence he afterwards withdrew, first to Leyden, and
then to the Hague. His ''Principles of Philosophy,''
in which he geometrically demonstrated the system
of Descartes, whilst opening out a new and original
field of metaphysics, aroused no less the wonder of
the learned than the animadversions of the orthodox
of every denomination. He afterwards published his
''Theologico-political Treatise,'' and ''Metaphysical
Meditations,'' and shortly after his death appeared
his posthumous works, including the celebrated
treatise on ''Ethics, geometrically demonstrated.''

Throughout all his works Spinoza exhibited wonderful depth of thought and close reasoning, but,
unfortunately, his propositions never lead up to any
result of practical utility, since he always chose as
the objects of his definitions those insoluble subjects,
which are beyond all human comprehension—the
Nature of the Deity, and the origin and destiny of
man. Though in active correspondence with most
of the greatest thinkers and many of the most illustrious personages of his day, he led a simple, obscure
life. Never a strong man, and subjected to a moral
persecution of the most galling kind, Spinoza died
at the Hague in 1677, in the forty-sixth year of his age.

Many other distinguished men might be mentioned, most of whose writings display much elegance of style, and deep religious feeling, but we can hardly find space to dwell upon them here. The material substance of the Spanish Jews played a part in the history of the times almost as important as their mental superiority. Many of the most important transactions of the age were worked out by means of funds furnished by Jewish capitalists, and among the undertakings so helped is to be included the expedition of William of Orange, which placed him on the British throne.

In conclusion we must cast a lingering regard on those unfortunate Jews who still remained in the Peninsula under the name of New Christians. The Inquisition, as we have seen, continued its fell course, and sat as a ghastly incubus on the thoughts and actions of men. The unhappy Marannos, outwardly the most devout among the whole Catholic population, continued to follow out in the depths of secrecy the observances of the old faith, despite the excessive peril with which this course was fraught. Informers were so largely benefited by their delations, and suspicion was so easily aroused, that no man felt safe from the detractions of the servants of his household, from secret enemies, or from unguarded friends. The utmost caution hardly secured the New Christians from the suspicion of showing signs of a tendency towards Judaism. Their habits, dress, and especially diet, were carefully noted down; their abstention from or manner of performing any Catholic rite, their conduct on Jewish sabbaths and festivals, their very looks and gestures were diligently watched, and often the slightest unintentional action was reported on, and the grim familiars of the Holy Court were heard knocking at the door, ready to carry off their unsuspecting victim to its dungeons for months, for years, perhaps for ever.

Thus passed on generation after generation of secret Jews, mingling with every grade of society, and filling every office of the State, and more especially of the Church, living in constant fear and trembling, still steadfast at heart, and from time to time yielding their steady tribute to the dungeon and the stake. Partly from the aversion of the people to mingle their blood with that of "the accursed seed of Israel," partly from the desire of the Marannos themselves to keep alive the remembrance of Judaism in their progeny, the New Christians generally intermarried among each other; but many were the occasions in which the bluest blood condescended to ally itself with heiresses of Hebrew lineage, so that there were few among the noblest families of Spain and Portugal who did not derive descent from Jewish ancestors. To so great an extent was this the case, that, when Joseph, King of Portugal, asked his great Minister Pombal, in the middle of the last century, whether he could not devise a peculiar hat to be worn, as a distinguishing mark, by the New Christians, to keep them separate from persons of "pure" blood, the great statesman brought three such hats to the king on the following day, and when asked for whom they were intended, he replied: "The one is for the Inquisitor-General, another for myself, and the third for your Majesty," thus indicating that Jewish blood flowed in the veins of all.

By means of constant emigration, however (and in 1629 a law was passed in Portugal, allowing secret Jews to leave the country), by unrelenting persecution, by intermarriage, and by the natural consequences of separation from the rest of their brethren, the Jews assimilated more and more with the rest of the population. All through the last century families of New Christians, in groups or singly, continued to find their way out of the Peninsula, and, after two hundred and more years of disguise, openly resumed Judaism; even in our own times isolated examples of the same circumstances are known to have happened. Since the beginning of the present century foreign Jews have been permitted to settle in Portugal, and there are now synagogues in Lisbon and two or three other cities; the Portuguese Inquisition, however, was only formally abolished in 1821, although it had long become practically inoperative.

In Spain, Napoleon put an end to the Holy Court in 1808; it was reopened, however, when Ferdinand VII. was restored, and the reaction set in, but finally the Inquisition was closed, let us hope for ever, in 1820. At this day there are probably no secret Jews in Spain or Portugal, for though there are still remote parts of Andalusia, and certain districts, especially in the neighbourhood of Braganza, where the greater part of the population is known to be of Jewish origin, and where still some lingering traditions of Hebrew observances can be traced, the meaning of such practices has now become lost, and they are merely recognised as customs of unknown significance handed down from preceding generations. Jews who settled in Spain are in these days in no way interfered with; but the establishment of a synagogue has not as yet been attempted, and would probably not be allowed, as, despite certain vague clauses in the constitution enjoining toleration, the spirit of the Inquisition still lingers in the minds of the people, and the edict of Ferdinand and Isabella has never been formally repealed.

CHRONOLOGICAL TABLE OF THE HISTORY OF THE JEWS IN SPAIN AND PORTUGAL

Prepared under Direction of David Bortin

Third Century C. E.—Evidence of Jewish settlements in Spain.

313   Council of Elvira disturbs friendly relations existing between Jews and Christians; intermarriage forbidden.

325   First Nicene Council separates the celebration of Easter from that of Jewish Passover.

339   Constantine forbids intermarriage and circumcision of slaves.

409   Vandal invasion of Spain.

412   Visigoths invade Spain.

485– 507   Alaric II rules Spain.

568– 586   Leovigild, Visigothic ruler of Spain.

586– 589   Reccared I, Visigothic King of Spain isolates Jews from Christians.

589   Third Council of Toledo. Catholicism made religion of the State.

612– 620   Isidore of Seville, most learned Spaniard of his time, criticizes anti-Jewish measures. Sisebut, Visigothic King, enacts forcible baptism or expulsion. 90,000 Jews embrace Christianity outwardly.

621– 631   Swinthila, successor of Sisebut; mild treatment encourages Jews to return to Spain. Baptized Jews openly profess Judaism again.

631– 636   Sisinand, Visigothic King, confirms decrees of Council of Toledo (633) forcing converts to Judaism back to Christianity; orders enslavement of baptized Jews practicing Jewish rites.

636– 640   Chintila (638) through sixth Council of Toledo enacts that only Catholics may reside in Visi-

	gothic Spain. Chindasivind, Visigothic king. Pseudo-Christians openly return to Judaism.
649– 672	Receswin II institutes more severe measures—Orders execution of Jews practicing Judaism.
653	Jews of Toledo promise to observe church regulations including eating of pork.
680– 687	Erwig, Visigothic king, enacts severe measures which twelfth Toledan Council accepts. Council presided over by Archbishop Julian of Toledo, himself of Jewish origin.
687– 701	Egica, Visigothic king, because Jews allied themselves with Arabs, orders all Jews sold into slavery and property confiscated (694).
701– 710	Witiza, Visigothic king; conflicting opinions regarding his treatment of Jews.
711– 715	Arab invasion of Spain; battle of Jerez (711). African Jews fight bravely under Kaulaal-Yahudi; Jewish inhabitants placed in charge of Cordova, Malaga, Granada, Seville, Toledo.
721	Appearance of false Messiah Serenus in Syria leads many Spanish Jews to emigrate to Palestine—Jews' property confiscated by Spanish Governor.
755– 788	Abd al-Rahman I, Mohammedan ruler; Jews prosper and attain prominence in services of Caliphate, in sciences, commerce, industry. Southern Spain becomes asylum for oppressed Jews.
910– 970	Menahem ben Saruk, founder of Judæo-Spanish culture.
912– 961	Abd al-Rahman II and Al-Hakem IX; golden era for Spanish Jews and Jewish science. Chasdai ibn Shaprut, court physician and patron of Jewish scholars.
960	Moses ben Enoch, appointed Rabbi of Cordova, Spain becoming center of Talmudic study.
920– 990	Dunash ibn Labrat, poet.
930– 950	Ramiro II, Christian King of Leon.
955	Chasdai negotiates treaty with Ordono III.
976–1013	Hisham II, ruler of Spain.
985–1040	Jonah ibn Janah, grammarian.
993–1056	Samuel ibn Nagdala, vizier at Granada.

1013 (Apr. 19) Massacre at Cordova by Sulaiman ibn al-Hakim.

1013–1103 Isaac al-Fassi, Rabbinical authority.

1019–1038 Habbus, ruler of Granada, friendly to Jews.

1021–1069 Solomon Ibn Gabirol, poet and philosopher.

1027–1065 Ferdinand I.

1038–1073 Badis, son of Habbus, ruler of Granada.

1050 Council of Coyanza revives Visigothic law forbidding Jews and Christians from living and eating together.

1055 Badis annexes Malaga.

1055–1066 Joseph son of Samuel Nagid, vizir at Granada.

1065–1109 Alphonso VI; tolerant attitude toward Jews praised by Pope Alexander II.

1066 (Dec. 30) Massacre of 1500 Jewish families at Granada. First persecution of Jews on Peninsula under Islamic rule. Banishment of Jews from Granada.

1069 Mutamid I, ruler of Seville.

1076 Alphonso VI grants Jews full equality with Christians.

1085 Pope Gregory VII protests to King of Castile against allowing Jews authority over Christians.

1086 Battle of Zallaka—Jews fight bravely in both Christian and Moorish armies. 40,000 Jews in Alphonso's army. Battle did not begin until after Sabbath.

1086 Yusuf ibn Tashfin of Northern Africa aids Moors at head of Almoravides a fanatical religious sect who become rulers of Southern Spain.

1086–1140 Judah ha-Levi, poet and philosopher.

1090 Alphonso VI decrees duels for settling litigation between Christian and Jew.

1092–1167 Abraham ibn Ezra, poet and exegete.

1095 First Crusade. (France.)

1106–1143 Ali, second Almoravide ruler; position of Jews in Southern Spain favorable.

1108 Massacre at Toledo.

1110–1180 Abraham ibn David, philosopher and historian.

1117 False Messiah appears at Cordova.

1126–1157   Alphonso VII very friendly to Jews of Leon, Toledo and San Diago.

1135   Birth of Moses Maimonides at Cordova.

1137   Barcelona joined to Aragon.

1139   Death of Moses ibn Ezra, liturgical poet.

1141   Judah ha-Levi migrates to Palestine.

1146   Beginning of Almohade persecution in North Africa and Southern Spain; Jews flee or pretend to accept Islam. Persecution continues for ten years.

1146–1147   Second Crusade.

1148   Cordova taken by Almohades.

1158–1214   Alphonso VIII, King of Castile. Jews gain influence and favor.

1162–1196   Alphonso II, King of Aragon.

1165–1173   Travels of Benjamin of Tudela.

1172   Perpignan joined to Aragon.

1178   Riot at Tòledo at which Fermosa, Jewish mistress of Alphonso VIII, is killed.

1188–1230   Alphonso IX, King of Leon.

1194–1270   Moses Nachmanides, Talmudist, exegete.

1196–1213   Peter II, King of Aragon.

1212   Jews of Toledo killed by Crusaders. First persecution of Jews in Castile.

1213   Ferdinand III; Castile and Leon united; turning point in Jewish history; clergy direct efforts against Jews. Innocent IV admonishes Ferdinand not to permit Jews to appear in public, without badge.

1213–1276   King James I, Aragon; Jews compelled to wear badges. Kings Ferdinand and James continue to grant favors to Jews despite clergy.

1233   Inquisition at Aragon.

1246   James I of Aragon declares Jews to be ''in commanda regis.''

1248   Conquest of Seville.

1248–1279   Alphonso III, King of Portugal.

1250–1328   Asher ben Jehiel, Talmudist.

1250   Bull of Innocent IV prohibits building of Synagogues without permission. Proselytizing forbidden on pain of death. Association with Christians forbidden. Severe restriction enacted; wearing badge enforced.

1252–1284   Alphonso X. Castile favorably disposed toward Jews. Famous astronomical tables ''Alphonsine Tables'' edited by Isaac ibn Sid of Toledo. Building of synagogue in Toledo.

1259   Jehudan de Cavalleria becomes treasurer of Aragon.

1263   Disputation at Barcelona between Pablo Christiani, and Nachmanides.

1273 (Nov. 4)   Jews of Lerida permitted to take oath on Ten Commandments instead of the oath of ''More Judaica.''

1279–1325   Diniz, King of Portugal.

1280   Alphonso X orders Jews of Leon and Castile imprisoned until payment of 12,000 moravides is made.

1281   Jews of Catalonia, Aragon, Valencia ordered to furnish 181,000 sueldos by King Pedro III.

1284–1295   Sancha IV of Castile abolishes legislative autonomy for Jews (1286).

1295–1312   Ferdinand IV, king of Castile.

1305   Ban against study of sciences.

1312–1350   Alphonso XI protects Jews against arbitrary enactments of violence.

1328   Massacres in Navarre.

1336–1387   Peter IV, King of Aragon.

1339   Algeciras taken.

1340–1410   Hasdai Crescas, philosopher.

1340   Death of Jacob, author of ''Tur.''

1348   Black Death.

1350–1369   Peter the Cruel, friendly to Jews; was derided as having a ''Jewish Court.'' Samuel Ha-Levi his chief.

1352–1435   Paul of Burgos, converted Jew; violent persecutor of Jews.

1360   Massacre of all Jews of Najeia by King's half brother Henry de Trastamara.

1366   Massacres in various places in Spain.

1369–1379   Henry II continues cruelties.

1379–1390   John I, King of Aragon.

1380   Cortes of Soria issues anti-Jewish enactments.
1385   Jews forbidden to live in Christian quarters.
                John I, King of Portugal.
1390–1406   Henry III. Very hostile. Imposes heavy taxes.
1391 (June 6)   Spanish horrors begin. Ferdinand Martinez
                incites the mob against Jews of Seville; anti-
                Jewish riots spread throughout Castile and Ara-
                gon. Turning point in History of Spanish Jews.
                Auto-da-Fé at Seville.
1403 (Oct. 25) Juan II of Castile withdraws civil jurisdic-
                tion from Jews.
1406   Burgos appointed executor of Henry III's will
                and guardian of John II.
1406–1454   John II.
1411   Vincent Ferrer rouses populace against Jews;
                second general massacre of Jews in all Spanish
                provinces. Many Jewish conversions by Ferrer.
1412   Every city enjoined to establish Morerias and
                Judarias surrounded by walls and one gate.
1412–1416   Ferdinand I, King of Aragon.
1413–1414   Disputation at Tortosa.
1415   Study of Talmud forbidden by Papal bull.
1437–1509   Isaac Abrabanel.
1440   Maranos of Toledo slain.
1454–1474   Henry IV, King of Castile. Position of Jews
                fairly favorable.
1458–1479   John II, King of Aragon. Conditions of Jews
                favorable.
1462   Cortes restricts Jews in their intercourse with
                Christians.
1467   Toledo riot.
1470   Carnage at Vaolladolid.
1473   Massacre of Maranos at Cordova. Jews offer to
                buy Gibraltar from Henry IV, as asylum.
1474   Attack on Maranos at Segovia. Only 12,000
                Jewish families left in Castile.
1474–1504   Isabella, Queen of Castile.
1479   Isabella marries Ferdinand of Aragon. Ferdi-
                nand a grandson of a Jewess.
1480   Jewish printing presses in Spain. Inquisition es-

tablished. Cortes of Toledo orders Jews to be confined to Ghettos at night.

1481 Jan. 6 The Inquisition against the Maranos established in Seville and other places at Castile.

1481-1495 John II, King of Portugal.

1482 Inquisition established in Aragon.

1483 Torquemada appointed Inquisitor General.

1486 Feb. 12 Auto-da-Fé at Toledo at which 740 were absolved.

Dec. 10 Auto-da-Fé at Toledo, 900 Jews ''reconciled.''

1488 May 24 Autos-da-Fé at Toledo. 21 Jews burned; 400 others punished.

July 30 6 Jews burned. Auto-da-Fé at Toledo.

1491 Granada surrenders.

1492 Aug. 2 Expulsion of Jews from Spain. Catholic sovereigns enter Moslem capital. Jews expelled from Castile and Aragon. Columbus discovers America.

1495–1521 Manoel I, King of Portugal.

1496 Jewish expulsion from Portugal. Manoel of Portugal orders the Jews to accept baptism or leave the country. Expulsion of Jews from Styria.

1498 The exiles settled in Navarre banished.

1501 (July) Fifty-four Jews burned at Seville.

1506 Massacre of 4000 Maranos in Lisbon.

1508 (July) Royal decree issued expelling Jews from Portugal.

1516 Charles V, King of Spain.

1521–1557 John III, King of Portugal.

1531 Clement VII issues bull establishing the Portuguese inquisition for Maranos.

1537 Jews of Portugal ordered to wear badges.

1548 July 10 Eighteen hundred Maranos released from the prisons of the Inquisition in Portugal.

1557–1578 Sebastian grants Jews free departure.

1588 Destruction of Spanish Armada.

1593 First Marano settlement in Holland made at Amsterdam under Jacob Tirado.

1612 Portuguese Jews granted right of asylum in Hamburg.

1620   Agitation for expulsion of Jews from Ibernian Peninsula.

1632 July 11 Auto-da-Fé at Madrid.

1646   Jews in Brazil side with Dutch in their war with Portuguese.

1654 July 8   Twenty-four Jews land at New Amsterdam from Brazil.

1680 June   Auto-da-Fé at Madrid.

1682 May 10   Auto-da-Fé at Lisbon.

1733 July 40 Jews from Lisbon arrive at Savannah, Ga.

1813 Feb. 22 Spanish Inquisition suppressed by the Cortes.

1814 July 21 Spanish Inquisition reinstated by Ferdinand VII.

1820   Jews admitted again at Lisbon.

1820 March 9 Revolution again abolishes Inquisition.

1823 Oct. 1   Counter revolution re-establishes Holy Office.

1826 Aug. 1   One Judaiser burnt at Valencia.

1834 July 15 Queen Regent, Maria Christina mother of Isabella II, finally abolishes Inquisition.

1868   Jews permitted to return to Spain when it became a Republic.

1869   Constitution of Spain proclaims freedom of religious belief.

1876   Constitution of Spain preserves principle of freedom of conscience and forbids religious services in public except those of Catholicism.

1883   Jewish refugees from Russia enthusiastically received in Madrid.

1913 April 19 Joseph and Mary Fels warmly welcomed by City of Ronda, at the Spanish Land Values Conference held there.

1914–1918   Jewish expatriates and others find refuge in Spain; Dr. Max Nordau among their number.

AUTOS-DA-FÉ CELEBRATED IN SPAIN

* Indicates that Jews were punished though number unknown.

Date	Place	Punished	Burnt	Date	Place	Punished	Burnt
May 10, 1484	Saragossa	4	..	Dec. 22, 1560	Seville	..	1
June 3, 1484	"	..	3	Sept. 13, 1560	Madrid	..	29
Dec. 20, 1485	"	..	2	Mar. 15, 1562	Murcia	..	1
Feb. 13, 1486	"	1	..	Mar. 20, 1562	"	16	..
Feb. 24, 1486	"	..	3	June 17, 1565	Toledo	1	..
Mar. 17, 1486	"	..	3	Nov. 6, 1569	Las Palmas	*	..
April 28, 1486	"	..	4	June 18, 1570	Toledo	7	..
May 21, 1486	"	7	..	1578	"	1	..
June 25, 1486	"	5	..	1591	"	..	24
June 30, 1486	"	..	3	1593	Seville	1	..
July 28, 1486	"	..	3	1598	Toledo	1	..
Aug. 6, 1486	"	5	..	Nov. 7, 1610	}Lograno	6	..
Sept. 24, 1486	"	..	..	Nov. 8, 1610	}		
Oct. 21, 1486	"	..	6	Oct. 15, 1619	Toledo	1	..
Nov. 29, 1486	"	..	11	Nov. 30, 1624	Seville	*	..
Dec. 15, 1486	"	..	1	Dec. 14, 1625	"	67	4
Dec. 17, 1486	"	..	1	Dec. 21, 1627	Cordova	71	..
Jan. 21, 1487	"	..	5	July 22, 1628	Seville	2	..
Jan. 15, 1487	Toledo	700	..	April 27, 1630	Toledo	1	..
Feb. 15, 1487	Saragossa	..	..	June 29, 1634	Cuenca	57	..
Mar. 15, 1487	Toledo	1000	..	June 22, 1636	Valladolid	28	..
May 7, 1487	"	22	..	1641	Toledo	1	..
May 20, 1487	Saragossa	..	9	April 17, 1644	Seville	1	..
Aug. 18, 1487	"	..	3	Aug. 2, 1644	Valladolid	1	..
Aug. 20, 1487	"	..	3	Feb. 24, 1647	Cordova	12	..
Dec. 8, 1487	"	..	..	Mar. 29, 1648	Seville	..	29
Feb. 10, 1488	"	..	4	Dec. 28, 1649	Toledo	..	3
Feb. 15, 1488	"	..	1	1649	Valladolid	..	1
July 30, 1488	Toledo	..	16	Jan. 1651	Toledo	..	63
Mar. 2, 1510	Las Palmas	3	..	Jan. 1, 1651	"	..	2
Mar. 2, 1511	Cuenca	..	..	Nov. 30, 1651	"	*	..
Feb. 24, 1526	Las Palmas	5	..	April 28, 1652	"	4	..
Mar. 13, 1537	Saragossa	..	1	Aug. 24, 1652	"	4	..
May 21, 1559	Valladolid	..	2	Nov. 3, 1652	"	2	..

101

AUTOS-DA-FÉ CELEBRATED IN SPAIN—*Continued*

Date	Place	Punished	Burnt	Date	Place	Punished	Burnt
Dec. 28, 1652	Toledo	*	..	Oct. 7, 1663	Toledo	*	..
May 11, 1653	"	*	..	June 29, 1665	Cordova	96	..
May 18, 1653	"	*	..	Feb. 22, 1665	Toledo	*	..
Aug. 10, 1653	"	*	..	June 7, 1666	Cordova	23	..
Aug. 31, 1653	"	8	..	June 15, 1666	Toledo	*	..
Mar. 15, 1654	"	7	..	1666	"	..	1
June 29, 1654	Cuenca	47	10	May 1, 1667	"	3	..
Sept. 27, 1654	Toledo	*	..	Oct. 30, 1667	"	3	..
Dec. 12, 1654	Granada	*	12	1669	Cordova	13	..
Mar. —, 1655	Compostella	..	1	April 7, 1669	Toledo	*	..
May 3, 1655	Cordova	78	..	Nov. 17, 1669	"	*	..
Oct. 31, 1655	Toledo	7	..	July 20, 1670	Cordova	21	..
Jan. 30, 1656	"	1	..	May 18, 1670	Toledo	*	..
Sept. 10, 1656	"	8	..	Oct. 19, 1670	"	*	..
Sept. 17, 1656	"	2	..	Sept. 6, 1671	"	*	..
Oct. 8, 1656	"	2	..	Sept. 11, 1672	"	*	..
Oct. 15, 1656	"	2	..	Feb. 11, 1674	"	*	..
1657	Cordova	..	1	Oct. 14, 1674	"	..	1
1657	"	13	..	Feb. 14, 1679	"	4	..
Feb. 11, 1657	Toledo	3	..	Dec. 17, 1679	"	5	..
Mar. 11, 1657	"	3	..	Oct. 6, 1680	"	5	..
May 6, 1657	"	3	..	Dec. 21, 1680	"	*	..
July 1, 1657	"	8	..	Sept. 29, 1681	"	*	..
Sept. 16, 1657	"	6	..	1683	Seville	..	1
Dec. 9, 1657	"	17	..	April 25, 1683	Toledo	*	..
Aug. 24, 1658	"	7	..	1684	Granada	..	..
May 9, 1659	"	*	..	May 22, 1684	Toledo	2	1
Sept. 7, 1659	"	*	..	April 1, 1685	"	1	..
Jan. 11, 1660	"	..	1	Aug. 18, 1686	"	3	..
Feb. 9, 1660	Cordova	13	..	Oct. 15, 1686	"	1	..
Mar. 19, 1660	"	*	..	April 13, 1687	"	1	..
April 11, 1660	} Seville	80	7	1689	Granada	..	..
April 13, 1660	}			July 2, 1691	Majorca	38	37
1660	Toledo	..	1	Nov. 9, 1692	Toledo	1	..
June 13, 1660	"	2	..	May 18, 1692	Seville	1	..
Sept. 26, 1660	Toledo	*	..	Feb. 7, 1694	Toledo	*	..
April 4, 1661	"	*	..	June 6, 1694	"	3	..
Aug. 8, 1661	"	*	..	May 8, 1695	"	3	2
Dec. 4, 1661	"	6	..	Sept. 22, 1695	"	1	..
Feb. 24, 1662	Cordova	38	..	Oct. 23, 1695	"	2	..
April 11, 1662	Toledo	*	..	July 29, 1696	"	1	..
May 6, 1663	Cordova	19	..	Sept. 16, 1696	"	2	..

Date	Place	Punished	Burnt
Mar. 17, 1697	Toledo	..	..
Nov. 29, 1699	Valladolid	Many	..
1700	Seville	1	..
Sept. 26, 1700	Toledo	*	..
Mar. 6, 1701	"	*	..
Oct. 30, 1701	"	3	..
May 21, 1702	"	2	..
Nov. 12, 1702	"	2	..
Mar. 18, 1703	"	2	..
Oct. 28, 1703	Seville	*	1
Sept. 8, 1704	Toledo	2	1
Nov. 22, 1705	"	..	1
Dec. 31, 1706	Valladolid	*	..
Sept. 27, 1711	Toledo	1	..
June 30, 1716	Seville	..	1
April 4, 1718	Cordova	5	..
June 29, 1718	Seville	1	..
July 25, 1720	"	..	1
May 18, 1721	Madrid	*	..
Mar. 19, 1721	Toledo	*	..
Nov. 30, 1721	Granada	58	..
Dec. 14, 1721	Seville	38	..
Feb. 22, 1722	Madrid	10	..
Feb. 24, 1722	Seville	11	..
Mar. 15, 1722	Toledo	..	..
Oct. 25, 1722	"	12	..
Mar. 15, 1722	"	7	..
April 12, 1722	Cordova	14	..
May 17, 1722	Murcia	36	..
June 19, 1722	Cuenca	18	..
July 5, 1722	Seville	43	..
Nov. 30, 1722	"	42	4
Nov. 30, 1722	Llerena	17	..
Jan. 31, 1723	Granada	54	..
Jan. 31, 1723	Barcelona	4	..
Jan. 31, 1723	Seville	54	12
June 6, 1723	"	31	2
June 6, 1723	Saragossa	21	..
June 13, 1723	Cordova	23	15
June 20, 1723	Granada	25	..
Oct. 24, 1723	"	25	..
Feb. 24, ——	Toledo	7	2

Place	Date	Punished	Burnt
Oct. 28, 1723	Toledo	6	..
Feb. 20, 1724	Madrid	20	3
Mar. 12, 1724	Valladolid	5	4
April 2, 1724	Valencia	5	..
April 23, 1724	Cordova	26	14
June 11, 1724	Seville	33	1
June 25, 1724	Granada	39	5
July 2, 1724	Cordova	6	..
July 23, 1724	Cuenca	8	..
Nov. 30, 1724	Murcia	8	2
Dec. 21, 1724	Seville	8	..
Jan. 14, 1725	Cuenca	9	2
Feb. 4, 1725	Llerena	4	..
Mar. 4, 1725	Cuenca	1	..
May 13, 1725	Granada	20	7
July 1, 1725	Toledo	5	1
July 1, 1725	Valencia	2	..
July 8, 1725	Valladolid	5	..
Aug. 24, 1725	Granada	9	..
Aug. 26, 1725	Llerena	10	..
Sept. 9, 1725	Barcelona	2	..
Oct. 21, 1725	Murcia	6	..
Nov. 30, 1725	Seville	10	3
Dec. 16, 1725	Granada	10	1
Mar. 31, 1726	Valladolid	2	..
Mar. 31, 1726	Murcia	6	..
May 12, 1726	Cordova	9	..
Aug. 18, 1726	Granada	7	..
Aug. 18, 1726	Llerena	..	1
Sept. 1, 1726	Barcelona	1	1
Sept. 17, 1726	Valencia	*	..
June 11, 1726	Toledo	2	..
Jan. 26, 1727	Valladolid	17	..
May 9, 1728	Granada	*	..
Oct. 10, 1728	"	5	..
May 3, 1730	Cordova	14	..
Mar. 4, 1731	"	6	..
Mar. 20, 1738	Toledo	*	..
Mar. 21, 1738	"	12	1
Dec. 21, 1738	"	1	..
June 13, 1745	Valladolid	3	1
Dec. 5, 1745	Cordova	2	..

Date	Place	Punished	Burnt	Date	Place	Punished	Burnt
July 13, 1749	Cordova	1	1	Dec. —, 1781	Seville	..	1
Nov. 22, 1753	Seville	*	..	Aug. 11, 1799	"	*	..
Dec. 13, 1753	"	1	..	Aug. 26, 1799	"	*	..
Jan. 11, 1756	Toledo	1	..	Feb. 27, 1817	"		
Dec. —, 1758	Seville	1	..	Aug. 1, 1826	Valencia	..	1

AUTOS-DA-FÉ CELEBRATED IN PORTUGAL

Only such listed where Jews were known to have been punished or burnt.

Date	Place	Date	Place
Oct. 23, 1541	Libson	Mar 5, 1624	Lisbon
1541	Evora	April 1, 1629	Evora
1543	Porto	Sept. 2, 1629	Lisbon
June 27, 1563	Goa	April 2, 1642	"
Dec. 5, 1563	"	Dec. 22, 1647	"
Oct. 27, 1564	"	Dec. 1, 1652	"
June 15, 1567	"	Dec. 15, 1658	Porto
Jan. 18, 1568	"	Oct. 17, 1660	Lisbon
Jan. 28, 1568	"	Mar. 12, 1673	Coimbra
July 17, 1569	"	May 10, 1682	Lisbon
April 22, 1571	"	Aug. 8, 1683	"
May 18, 1574	"	Aug. —, 1701	"
Sept. 4, 1575	"	Mar. 2, 1704	Coimbra
Oct. 28, 1576	"	Sept. 6, 1705	Lisbon
Sept. 1, 1577	"	Dec. 6, 1705	"
Aug. 17, 1578	"	July 25, 1706	Evora
Sept. 6, 1579	"	June 30, 1707	Lisbon
Dec. 4, 1580	"	July 9, 1713	"
Dec. 14, 1582	"	June 17, 1718	Coimbra
Nov. 10, 1585	"	Mar. 14, 1723	"
Sept. 13, 1587	"	Oct. 10, 1723	Lisbon
Aug. 3, 1603	Lisbon	Oct. 13, 1726	"
Mar. 27, 1605	Evora	Sept. 1, 1739	"
Mar. 24, 1606	"	Oct. 18, 1739	"
Oct. 17, 1610	"		

AUTOS-DA-FÉ CELEBRATED IN AMERICA

Lima	Cartagena de Las Indias	Mexico
Nov. 15, 1573	Feb. 2, 1614	1524–26
April 1, 1578	July —, 1618	1536
Oct. 29, 1581	Mar. 13, 1622	1539*
Nov. 30, 1587	Jan. 17, 1626	1549
April 5, 1592	Aug. 6, 1627	1555
Dec. 17, 1595	June 25, 1628	1558
Dec. 10, 1600	Mar. 7, 1632	1560
Mar. 13, 1605	Mar. 26, 1634	1561
June 1, 1608	June 1, 1636	1562
June 17, 1612	Mar. 25, 1638	1569
Dec. 21, 1625	July 22, 1642	Feb. 28, 1574
Feb. 27, 1631	May 24, 1648	Mar. 6, 1575
Aug. 11, 1635	Nov. 28, 1649	Feb. 19, 1576
Aug. 17, 1635	Dec. 21, 1650	Dec. 15, 1577*
Jan. 23, 1639	April 25, 1653	1578*
Nov. 17, 1641	July 22, 1653	1579*
Jan. 23, 1664	April 28, 1654	1579–90
Feb. 16, 1666	May 8, 1655	1590*
June 28, 1667	June 6, 1655	1591
Oct. 8, 1667	Oct. 1, 1656	1592*
Mar. 16, 1693	Sept. 16, 1657	1594
Oct. 8, 1694	May —, 1669	1595
Nov. 28, 1719	Mar. 2, 1670	Dec. 8, 1596*
Dec. 21, 1720	Aug. 24, 1671	Mar. 26, 1601*
1728	Sept. 4, 1671	1603*
July 12, 1733	Sept. 4, 1672	1606
Dec. 23, 1736	Feb. 17, 1675	1608
Nov. 11, 1737	April 4, 1677	1621
Oct. 19, 1749	Oct. 23, 1678	1625*
April 6, 1761	Nov. 12, 1679	1626*
Sept. 1, 1773	Dec. 21, 1681	1630*
1776	Oct. 28, 1682	1635*

Lima	Cartagena de Las Indias	Mexico
Feb. 18, 1800	July 29, 1683	1636*
Aug. 27, 1803	Aug. 29, 1683	Jan. 23, 1639
Sept. 10, 1805	Feb. 11, 1685	1645*
July 17, 1806	Sept. 9, 1685	1646*
	May 30, 1688	1647*
	Dec. 11, 1689	1648*
	April 29, 1691	1648*
	Mar. —, 1695	1649*
	April 27, 1697	1652
	April 29, 1699	Oct. 29, 1656
	Jan. 10, 1700	Nov. 19, 1659*
	June 20, 1700	May 4, 1664
	Feb. 24, 1707	Dec. 7, 1664
	Mar. 18, 1708	1690
	May 21, 1708	(Baxaca)
	May 26, 1711	Jan. 15, 1696
	July 9, 1713	Mar. 20, 1679
	July 29, 1714	1704
	June 11, 1715	1708
	Nov. 30, 1715	1712*
	June 20, 1717	1722
	Feb. 5, 1782	Sept. 6, 1767
		Mar. 13, 1768
		Aug. 9, 1795*
		Nov. 26, 1814
		1815

* Indicates where Jews were known to have been punished or burnt.